FUNCTIONING IN ENGLISH

Communicatively-Based Units for the Teaching of Speaking

David Mendelsohn
Rose Laufer
Jūra Seskus

(University of Toronto)

Hodder & Stoughton Limited

IN ASSOCIATION WITH

Dominie Press Limited

Editorial Consultants

Professor Mary Ashworth
Jean Handscombe

The original version of six of
these Units was commissioned by
and prepared for The School of
Continuing Studies, University
of Toronto.

ISBN 0-340-35708-8 (Hodder & Stoughton)
ISBN 0-88751-019-1 (Dominie)

PUBLISHED BY

Hodder and Stoughton Limited
in association with
Dominie Press Limited

DISTRIBUTED BY

Dominie Press Limited
1361 Huntingwood Drive, Unit 7
Agincourt, Ontario, M1S 3J1
Canada

Cover Design: Victoria Hunt Shannon
Text Illustrations: Lisa Figueroa
Typeset By: Algotext Inc.

Printed in Canada
Second Printing 1988
Third Printing 1989

INTRODUCTION — TO THE TEACHER

1. **The Purpose of the Book**

FUNCTIONING IN ENGLISH is a text that provides a large number of activities, divided into ten Units for the speaking component of an ESL/EFL course. It is designed to train the student to function effectively in what we consider to be the main types of communication that he/she needs at this level: to request and give information, to request and give directions, to express likes and dislikes, to make suggestions, to make small talk, to express agreement and disagreement, to describe, to give opinions, to persuade, to develop an idea, and to interrupt.

While the book is for use in the speaking part of a course, a great many of the activities can and should be integrated with work in the other skill areas, and a number of activities lend themselves to follow-up work in the writing class in particular. Writing activities directly related to this material are suggested in a number of Units in the Teacher's Manual.

2. **Whom FUNCTIONING IN ENGLISH is Intended for**

This book is intended for use by adults and young adults. The level of proficiency may be described as "Intermediate" in a three-part proficiency classification of Elementary-Intermediate-Advanced. It is too advanced for complete beginners in the language, and throughout the book we have presupposed mastery of a basic core of language.

3. **The Basic Philosophy Underlying the Book**

FUNCTIONING IN ENGLISH aims at teaching the Intermediate level student to communicate. It comes as a response to the two questions we posed for ourselves before beginning the book: (1) What do our students need to be able to do (i.e. express) in English, and (2) How can we facilitate this? The answer to the first question is to be found in the ten communicative functions that make up the ten Units of the book.

The material presented in each Unit is intended to answer the second question: How can we facilitate this? The book is built on the premise that spoken communication, which is our goal, is part of something broader — social interaction. As such, language must be seen as being governed not only by linguistic rules (grammar, phonology, etc.) but also by sociolinguistic rules (setting, topic, relationship between speakers, etc.), which determine the effectiveness, appropriateness and perceived meaning of any chunk of language. *FUNCTIONING IN ENGLISH* is committed to the inseparability of these two dimensions, and language forms are seen as successfully conveying a particular meaning only if the language is linguistically *and sociolinguistically* correct. For example, in Unit III, students are trained to express likes and dislikes, not in a vacuum, but in a way that befits their relationship with the person they are speaking to (e.g. were they courteous/formal enough?), and their intent (e.g. did they mean to be as strongly opposed to/in favor of something as native speakers would interpret them as being?).

A further dimension of recognizing spoken communication as part of social interaction is the recognition that most of our speaking is *dialog* (i.e. interaction) with one or more persons, and that we seldom give prolonged monologs. This, too, is reflected in the materials presented in most of the Units in the book. However, this could result in students not getting any practice at all in speaking in more than short utterances ("short turns") and as a result, Unit X, *Developing an Idea*, is committed to teaching them to speak in "longer turns".

While the book aims at teaching the students to carry out these ten communicative functions successfully, we are aware of the fact that at the Intermediate level, only certain aspects, and only certain linguistic realizations of, say, "requesting", can and should be covered. This resulted in a need to select the most useful features and forms, with the hope that teachers will "spiral back" to these same functions at a higher level and deal with some of the more sophisticated aspects.

4. *The Lay-out*

There is a Student Book accompanied by a Teacher's Manual.

The book is divided into ten Units:

Unit I   — Requesting and Giving Information
Unit II   — Requesting and Giving Directions
Unit III   — Part A: Interrupting
             Part B: Expressing Likes and Dislikes
Unit IV   — Making Suggestions
Unit V   — Making Small Talk
Unit VI   — Agreeing and Disagreeing
Unit VII   — Describing
Unit VIII — Giving Opinions
Unit IX   — Persuading
Unit X   — Developing an Idea

5. *The Structure of the Unit*

Each of the Units is made up of some initial presentation of forms conveying the function in question, followed by a number of activities. The activities may, for some programs, be too numerous. In such cases certain of the activities can be omitted. The decision as to what to omit must rest with the teacher, determined by the particular class she is teaching. However, some broad description of the structure of a Unit will be helpful. It must be noted that the Units are not identical in format (a deliberate attempt to obviate monotony), and so the following description should be seen only as providing a broad sense of the structure.

The materials are designed according to two basic principles that we believe in when teaching speaking: (i) If students are to learn how to speak, they have to be given a lot of practice in speaking; (ii) The speaking component of a program should not merely provide time and opportunities to speak, but it should also teach students *how* to communicate.

Units usually begin with a list of terms and expressions central to conveying a communicative meaning (e.g. describing). This is sometimes presented as a list, and then followed by some controlled activities aimed at providing exemplification and practice in using them. It is at this stage that the necessary grammatical forms are generally pointed out and should be taught or reviewed by the teacher. In some Units, so as to break the pattern, the Unit begins with key terms and expressions immediately presented in a context — this, too, is followed by some controlled activity providing practice in using these terms.

The next phase of the Unit is less-controlled activities and/or "consciousness-raising" activities. Students are gradually being required to effectively communicate the function in question. Considerable time is devoted at this stage to activities that will make the student aware of some of the sociolinguistic features of successful communication that are so vital to being correctly interpreted: the interpersonal relationship that exists between speakers, the mood, the degree of tentativeness/directness that is called for under these circumstances, etc. Such features are not universal. The way they operate in another language may be (and often is) different from the way they operate in English. Consequently, we have devised activities that bring this awareness to a conscious level. These activities *include discussion* of how a particular communicative effect was created.

The final phase of each Unit is a number of free activities to provide practice in the function that has been taught in as real a way as possible.

6. *The Modular, Flexible Format*

The book has been written in such a way as to give the teacher maximum flexibility. Certain classes might not need all the activities and may in fact already know the point being taught. In such cases, those activities should be omitted.

The Units are constructed in modular form and are not presented in any binding order, and may be successfully used in any order that the teacher chooses.

However, our classroom testing of this material has suggested some guides:

a) Unit I — *Requesting and Giving Information* is linguistically and sociolinguistically the simplest, most basic Unit in the book.

b) Part A of Unit III — *Learning to Interrupt* can be dealt with at any point. However, we found that it needs to be taught along with the first of the Units that might call for effective, successful interrupting, so that if a teacher decides, for example, to teach Unit IX (Persuading) very early on, we would advise teaching Interrupting then, and not leaving it until teaching Unit III.

c) Unit X — *Developing an Idea* is not devoted to a communicative function of the same type as those in Units I to IX. It is aimed at training students to be able to talk in more than single utterances — in "longer turns."

As we have said, training students to communicate in interactions carries with it the danger of failing to train them to be able to develop a longer piece of spoken discourse. This Unit is designed to practice talking in "longer turns." It therefore is a fairly sophisticated Unit, and we would advise placing it towards the end of the course.

7. *The Teacher's Manual*

Each Unit begins with a working definition of the communicative function as it has been defined and limited for the purposes of this Intermediate level text.

Activities that require "answers" have the answers provided in the Teacher's Manual, along with careful notes of explanation.

Details of the linguistic forms and sociolinguistic variables, and the sociolinguistic rules at work along with the linguistic rules, are discussed at length, particularly in relation to the "consciousness-raising" activities.

The Teacher's Manual also contains suggestions as to how and where the use of a video-recorder, tape-recorder or "teletrainer" would be useful. Natural speed of delivery and natural intonation should be used by the teacher throughout.

Comments related to paralinguistic features such as gesture, eye-contact, loudness of voice, etc., are made where appropriate. We believe that paralinguistics is an integral part of communication — that it comes either to reinforce and complement what is being said in words (e.g. body movement accompanying and emphasizing stressed syllables), or in place of words (e.g. a nod of the head meaning "I agree"). Students have to be made aware of the important role paralinguistics (body language, gesture, eye-contact, facial expression, loudness/softness, voice quality, etc.) play in being correctly interpreted when speaking. They have to realize, for example, that a set of words with one facial expression can have a totally different communicative value when said in the same way, but with a different facial expression. They have to learn that paralinguistic features can heighten or soften the intensity of what is being said.

On the other hand, we do not believe that there is an "inventory" of paralinguistic features that should be taught actively as a necessary ingredient of a particular communicative function. For this reason, paralinguistics is handled in terms of comments and suggestions to the teacher, particularly in the "consciousness-raising" parts of the Units, and there are no activities specifically designed to practice the production of paralinguistic features.

Reference is also made to Attending Skills (the skills of being a good listener in an interaction), since these, too, are very important in real communication.

8. *On-going Activities*

(a) As has been explained, the book is modular so as to be maximally flexible. However, there are a few activities that can be "on-going" throughout the course, in that one or two students may be involved each lesson (e.g. a two-minute news/weather report daily). These are listed below so that the teacher can decide at the beginning of the course, which of these to use, and when to begin them.

The following are the "on-going" activities:
   1) Unit VII, Activity 4
   2) Unit X,   Activity 4
   3) Unit X,   Activity 8

(b) In addition to the above, the teacher should include speaking activities unrelated to the function at hand. This will provide variety and opportunities for speaking without having to be anxious about a particular linguistic or sociolinguistic point.

9. *The Usefulness of the Book in Any Country*

A book such as *FUNCTIONING IN ENGLISH*, which teaches speaking as a part of social interaction, cannot operate in a vacuum. Utterances become (and may be judged as) effective communication only in terms of when and where they are located. Consequently, in the instances in which "place" is central, for example in Unit II, certain maps are provided. In addition, there are detailed explanations in the Teacher's Manual as to how to do the activity in question, but using local maps if the teacher prefers.

10. *Reference to the Teacher in the Student Book in the Teacher's Manual*

Throughout the book, the pronouns "she" and "her" are used when referring to the teacher. This is intended to be the generic *she* and is in no way an indication of the sex of the teacher — it simply obviates the very clumsy forms such as: He/she then introduces himself/herself to his/her students.

11. *Notation Used in the Student Book*

When listing key words and expressions, two forms of notation have been used that require clarification:

(a) A word in a set of brackets = an optional additional word
    e.g. It's (probably) true that . . .
        I'm not (very) fond of . . .

(b) A slash between words = opposites or "sets" of words
    e.g.Turn right/left.
        Go north/south/east/west.

CONTENTS

FOR BENJAMIN

ACKNOWLEDGEMENTS

We would like, first and foremost, to thank Marian Tyacke, our friend and Department Head, for her enthusiasm, encouragement and support. We would also like to thank Duncan Green, Harry Mills and Warren Jevons, the Directorate of The School of Continuing Studies at the University of Toronto, for their assistance in making this book happen.

A special word of thanks is also due to our many colleagues who piloted the materials, to our friends whom we have had to neglect, and to May Bierman for her outstanding dedication in deciphering and typing.

Finally, Jack, Aldona, Jenny, Lee, Anna and Jonathan, your understanding and patience made it all possible!

David Mendelsohn
Rose Laufer
Jūra Seskus
Toronto, August 1983

TO THE STUDENT

FUNCTIONING IN ENGLISH is a book designed to help you learn how to speak English. It is written especially for adults and young adults.

There are ten Units, and each one teaches the types of things that we have found that our students need and want to be able to say. The book teaches you:

(a) how to ask for information you need;

(b) how to give information when you are asked;

(c) how to ask for and to tell how to get to a place;

(d) how to say when you like something and when you don't like something in an acceptable way for an English-speaking culture;

(e) how to suggest things to people even when they may not agree with you;

(f) how to "chat" to people — because English speaking people will think you're unfriendly if you keep quiet;

(g) how to agree and disagree with people, being as polite or direct as you mean to be;

(h) how to describe things in words;

(i) how to give your opinion without people thinking you are being rude or "pushy";

(j) how to persuade in English (it might be quite different from what you do in your language);

(k) how to talk for several minutes and develop an idea;

(l) how to interrupt successfully and politely in English.

This is not a "Grammar" book — it is not a book for practicing and doing grammar exercises. It is a book for *learning how to say what you want to say.*

When learning to say what you mean, you have to think of many things such as: Who am I speaking to? Am I being too direct? Am I making my point too strongly? We have tried in this book to show you how "social language rules" work in English and to give you practice in them.

In summary, after studying from *FUNCTIONING IN ENGLISH*, you should be better able to function in English!

Good Luck!

THE AUTHORS

David Mendelsohn received his B.A. and TESL Certificate from the Hebrew University of Jerusalem and Ph.D. in Applied Linguistics from Edinburgh University. He has taught in Applied Linguistics and ESL and trained ESL teachers. He is currently at the University of Toronto.

Rose Laufer received her B.A. in Linguistics and TESOL Certificate from the University of Toronto. She has taught in Cuba, McGill and Concordia Universities. She is currently a Master Teacher of ESL at the University of Toronto.

Jūra Seskus received her B.A. in Linguistics and TESL Certificate from the University of Toronto, her B.Ed. from the Ontario Teacher's College and her M.Sc. in Applied Linguistics from Edinburgh University. She has trained ESL teachers and taught ESL at the University of Toronto and Centennial College. She is currently teaching at the Gulf Polytechnic in Bahrain.

UNIT I. REQUESTING AND GIVING INFORMATION

Activity 1. Breaking the Ice

"Breaking the ice" is an idiom that means getting to know someone. An atmosphere that was cold becomes warm. Now we will break the ice here by seeing how well we can remember each other's names.

We will sit in a circle and the teacher will start. The teacher says: "I am Linda, the teacher, from Canada." The person to her left says: "I am taking an English course. In my class there is Linda, the teacher from Canada, and Dennis (himself) from Hong Kong." The next person has to repeat all that Dennis said, plus the information about himself/herself, and so on, all the way round the class.

Activity 2. Introducing Yourself

A. When you meet someone for the first time, it is customary to introduce yourself.
   Some expressions used:

   My name is . . . /My name's . . .
   I'm . . .
   First name
   Last name
   Hi
   Hello
   How do you do?

   Go over this dialog:

   Chong: Hello. Are you a student here?
     Ami: Yes, I am.
   Chong: So am I. My name's Chong Yong.
     Ami: How do you do? I'm Ami Frank.
   Chong: I'm pleased to meet you. Is Frank your first name or your last name?
     Ami: My last name.
   Chong: Chong's my first name. Please call me Chong.
     Ami: Okay, Chong, and please call me Ami.
   Chong: Okay, Ami.

B. Now form a double circle, and introduce yourself to the person facing you. The outside circle will move to the right, while the inner circle stays in place. Shake hands and smile when introducing yourself.

Activity 3.   Preparing to Introduce Someone

Here are some expressions used when we want to introduce someone:

I'd like to introduce . . .

I'd like you to meet . . .

Can I introduce you to . . .

Quan, this is Rodolfo.

The purpose of this activity is to get information about another person, and then introduce him/her to the class. You will be working in pairs. Here are some questions to use. Let's go over them before you start:

1. What's your name?
2. Where are you from?/What country are you from?
3. Do you work?
4. If not, what do you do?
5. Are you married?
6. When did you arrive here?
7. What language do you speak at home?
8. Do you have a hobby?
9. What are three things you like and three things you don't like?

If there is any other information you would like to add, you may do so. It's a good idea to take some notes so that you will remember all the points.

When the class gets together again, you will introduce your partner to the class and tell the class about him/her.

Activity 4.   Getting and Giving Information about a Country

Some expressions used in information about a country:

map	north (northern)
country	south (southern)
province (provincial)	east (eastern)
territory	west (western)
capital (capital city)	central
state	Atlantic Ocean
What is the capital of . . . ?	Pacific Ocean
border	federation (federal)
	Gulf of Mexico

A. We will go over the names of the provinces/states and capital cities on your map.

B. Now that you are familiar with the names, fill in the blank map with:
    1. The names of certain provinces, territories and states.
    2. The capitals of certain provinces, territories and states.

C. Let's learn how to talk about where places are located:

        Where is Quebec in relation to Manitoba?
        Quebec is *east of* Manitoba.
        Where is Illinois in relation to Indiana?
        Illinois is *west of* Indiana.

    Other expressions:

        Toronto is (located) on Lake Ontario.
        Montreal is north-east of Toronto.
        Albany is the capital of New York State.
        Canada borders on the United States.
        The 49th parallel divides the U.S.A. and Canada.
        Utah is between Nevada and Colorado.

You will make up five questions about the map and then work in pairs. You will ask your partner questions and vice versa. Make sure you use the appropriate expressions.

Activity 5. Where I Come From

You are going to give a short talk about your country. Prepare this activity at home. If there is more than one person from the same country, then each of you should talk about a different aspect of your home country (e.g. climate, national customs, food or religion). Prepare your notes IN POINT FORM ONLY. This is a "talk," not a reading.

As each person gives his/her talk, the other students may ask questions or ask for more information.

Activity 6.   Shopping Project

You are going out of the classroom to use the English you have learned. You should get some information in different types of stores.

Some expressions:

A. *If the clerk speaks first:*   *Response:*
  1. May I help you?
  2. What can I do for you?   Yes please, I'd like to know how
                                        much X costs.
  3. Yes? (Yeah?)
  4. Would you like some help?
  5. What would you like?
  6. Can I help you?
  7. Are you looking for something?

B. *If you speak first:*
  1. Excuse me, could you please tell me . . .
  2. I wonder if you could help me. I'd like to know . . .
  3. I wonder if you could tell me . . .
  4. Excuse me, how much is X?

Now, you will be divided into groups. The information you will get will depend on which group you are in. Some questions will be the same for all groups.

Groups A,B,C — Go to a Supermarket.   *Groups D,E,F — Go to a Drug Store.*

Find out the prices of: *Find out the prices of:*

(a) water glasses   (a) nose drops

(b) light bulbs (60 W)   (b) baby powder

(c) a dozen oranges   (c) an alternative to aspirin (because

(d) a dozen eggs   you are allergic to aspirin)

    (large eggs)   (d) a brand of shampoo that you like

(e) a jar of jam   (e) a bar of bath soap

All groups

1. Find out the prices of your items in another store, and compare.
2. Choose an item that you would like to buy, and find out where it is sold and how much it sells for.
3. Would you like to do your regular shopping at the first store? Why?

Tomorrow each group will report their information to the class, and the groups will compare results.

Activity 7.   Requesting Information over the Telephone

Some useful expressions:

1. Could you please tell me . . .
2. Is this the Sales Department?
3. I would like some information about . . .
4. What is the best (cheapest, quickest, etc.) way to . . .
5. I'd like to speak to . . .

Sample Dialog:

Movie Theater Manager: Universal Theater.

John: Could you please tell me the times the movie starts?

Manager: It starts at 7:00 p.m. and there is a second show starting at 9:50.

John: Thank you.

Work in pairs. First think of a situation and then prepare a telephone dialog requesting information.

For homework, each of you will have some specific information to get on the telephone. You will report your information to the class tomorrow.

UNIT II. REQUESTING AND GIVING DIRECTIONS

Activity 1.   Using a Map of the Downtown Area

Key words and Expressions

When we want to ask for or give directions, we use the following expressions:

Questions:

Excuse me, where is the X theater?
Can/could you please tell me where the X theater is?
How do I get to the X theater?
I wonder if you could tell me where the X theater is?
Excuse me, the X theater is near here, isn't it?

Responses:

Yes, it's . . .
Sure, it's . . .
Not exactly; it's . . .
No, it's . . . .
(I'm) sorry, I don't know.
I'm new here as well.
I'm not sure.

Possible instructions:

Turn right/left.
Walk two lights east/west.
Cross Government St.
Three blocks north/south.
Go along this road.
Then turn right at the first lights.
Keep on this road until you reach Rose Ave.
At the corner, turn left.
Finally, go straight down/along the road until number 155.
Go over these expressions and make sure you know what they mean.

A Downtown Map

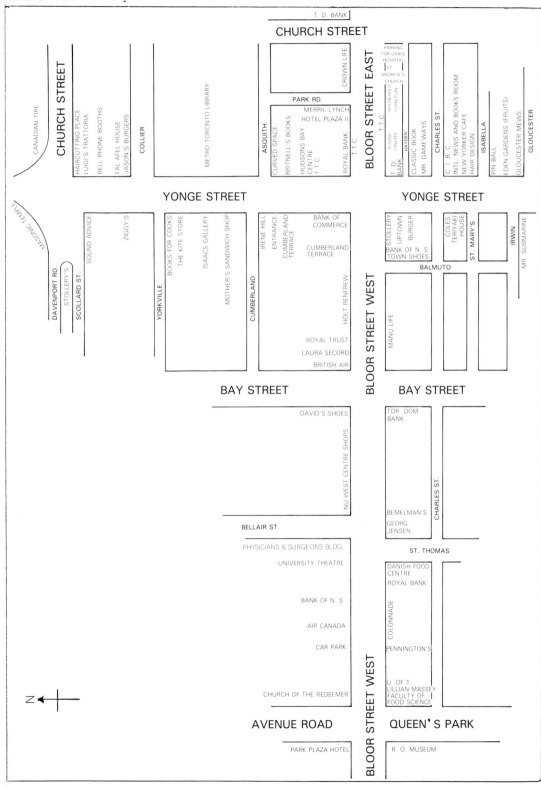

Here are some dialogs using expressions for requesting and giving directions. These dialogs take place at the corner of Bloor St. and Avenue Rd., on the north side. Look at your map and follow along.

1. Sofia: Excuse me. Could you tell me how I get to the Uptown theater from here?
    Bob: Yes. You cross Bloor St. and walk four blocks east and then make a right turn at Yonge St.
    Sofia: Is it south on Yonge St.?
    Bob: Yes, it is.
    Sofia: Thanks a lot.
    Bob: You're welcome.

2. Alain: Excuse me. How would I get to the Uptown theater from here?
    Sulla: I'm sorry. I'm new in town. I don't know.
    Alain: That's okay.

$$* \quad * \quad *$$

Once again, follow along on the map but this time see where you end up if you follow these directions.

1. Start at the Royal Ontario Museum (R.O.M.).
    First, go to the corner of Queen's Park and Bloor Street; then turn right on Bloor Street and go east. Walk four blocks east.
    Turn right at "Stollery's" and walk four blocks south.
    ### WHERE ARE YOU EXACTLY?

2. You are on the corner of Church St. and Yonge St. in front of "Canadian Tire." Walk three blocks south and cross the street. Then turn right.
    ### WHERE ARE YOU EXACTLY?

3. Start at "Pinball" (the corner of Yonge St. and Isabella St.).
    Cross Yonge Street and walk two blocks along St. Mary's St.
    Then turn right and walk up two blocks.
    Cross the street again, and walk one block west.
    ### WHERE ARE YOU EXACTLY?

Now prepare a set of directions similar to the ones above. Be ready to tell them to the class and have the class follow along. Did they correctly guess where your directions led them? Were your directions clear?

Activity 2. Learning about the Transit System

Key Words and Expressions

Here are some words and expressions we use when we talk about going somewhere using public transportation.

map
ride
guide
north
south
east
west
northbound
southbound
token
ticket
automatic entrance
ticket collector
conductor
exit
station
transfer
parallel

Make sure you know what these mean and then try using them in a sentence about a transit map of your area.

Activity 3. Using the Map of Marleetown

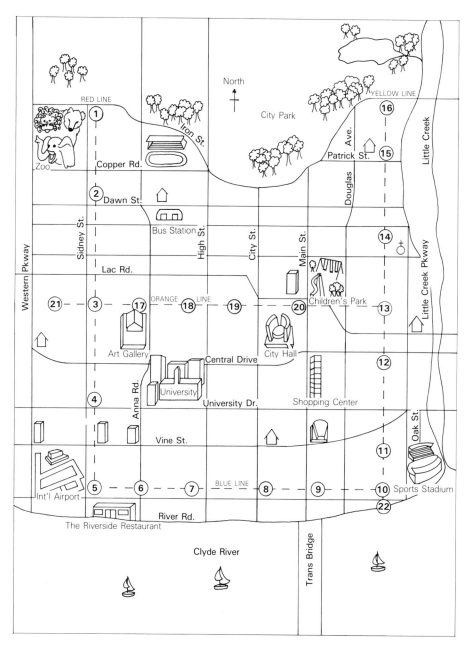

Legend:

Stations

1. Iron
2. Copper
3. Lac
4. University
5. Airport
6. Anna
7. Jonathan
8. City
9. Main
10. Eastern
11. Stadium
12. Central
13. Little Creek
14. Dawn
15. Patrick
16. Iron East
17. Gallery
18. High
19. Queen
20. Walnut
21. Lee
22. Clyde

Symbols

⌂ school
◯ subway station
– – – subway line (Orange, Blue, Yellow, and Red)
——— streets

Activity 3. Using the Map of Marleetown

In groups, find the answers to these questions using the map of Marleetown.

Group A:

1. What is the northernmost street on the map?
2. Find the Zoo on the map and tell which part of the city it is in.
3. Find a school on the map and say where it is.
4. Find Walnut station on the map and tell us where it is.
5. What is the nearest subway station to the Sports Stadium?
6. If you are at Iron Street and Anna Road, how do you get to the City Park?

Group B:

1. If you keep travelling south on the map, where do you end up?
2. Find the International Airport and tell which part of the city it is in.
3. Which is the westernmost station?
4. Find Queen station and tell us where it is.
5. Name the northernmost station on the Yellow subway line.
6. If you are at City Hall, how do you get to the Bus Station?

Group C:

1. What is the western boundary of the city?
2. Find the Shopping Center and say which part of the city it is in.
3. Where is the Children's Park?
4. Find Jonathan station and tell us where it is.
5. What is the most centrally located subway station?
6. If you are at Queen station, how do you get to the International Airport?

Group D:

1. What is the easternmost street on the map?
2. Find the University on the map and tell us which part of the city it is in.
3. Find the subway station closest to Vine Street.
4. Find Eastern station and tell us where it is.
5. Which is the best subway station to get off for the Shopping Center?
6. If you are at the Zoo and want to get to City Hall, which route is the most direct?

Activity 4. Getting Help from the Bus Driver

Sometimes we need to ask for help. Here are some dialogs showing how you can do so.

Key: A — the point where you are when you ask the driver for help.
  X — the point you *want* to get to.
  Y — the point that the bus goes to.
  → — the direction you are travelling in when you ask the driver for help.

14

Sample Dialog 1

⟶ A-------Y-----X-----

Passenger: Does this bus go to X?
Driver: No, we only go as far as Y. You will have to get off at Y and catch another bus there.
Passenger: Thanks very much.
Driver: You're welcome.

Sample Dialog 2

Y------A----- ⟵-------X----

Passenger: Does this bus go to X?
Driver: You're going in the wrong direction. This bus is going to Y. You'll have to get off at the next stop, cross over to the other side of the street, and catch a bus in the opposite direction. I'll give you a transfer.
Passenger: Thanks very much.
Driver: You're welcome.

Now, you try making up dialogs like the ones above, using the information given below.

Situation 1:

Lawrence Avenue

X   Y   ⟵   A

Lawrence station   Andrew station

You are on a bus that goes to Andrew station. You want to get to Lawrence station.

Situation 2:

Mills Road

Y   ⟵   A   X

Steel Ave.   The Science Center

You are on a bus that goes to Steel Avenue. You want to get to the Science Center.

Situation 3:

Eglinton Avenue

Y   ⟵   A   X

Eglinton station   York station

You are on a bus that goes to Eglinton station.
You want to get to York station.

Situation 4:

Grange Road

X   Y   ⟵   A

High St.   Lauder Rd.

You are on a bus that goes as far as Lauder Road.
You want to go to High Street.

Situation 5:   Green Street

        Y _____ X _____ < ____ A _____

        Bus Terminal   The Globe

You are on the Green St. bus and you want to go to the Globe.

Activity 5. Places of Interest

You will be put in one of the groups below and will work on that place of interest. Working with the map of Marleetown, discuss among yourselves what it is about this place that makes it interesting to visit. Then work out a way to get there from your starting point. Having finished that, write a dialog between three people in which the first person wants to go and visit something interesting; the second person tells him a little about it and tells him roughly where it is; then the second person asks the third person for exact directions. Be ready to present your dialog to the class.

	Starting Point	*Place of Interest*
Group A:	a house on the corner of Vine St. and Anna Rd.............	the City Park
Group B:	the Riverside Restaurant on River Rd. on the west side...........	the Children's Park
Group C:	a house on Main St. near the City Park.....	the International Airport
Group D:	the corner of Main St. and Lac Rd.........	the Zoo
Group E:	the corner of Patrick St. and Douglas Ave..............	the Sports Stadium

Activity 6. Apartment Plan

Here are some words we need to know in order to describe floor plans of rooms, apartments, and houses:

Rooms and Furnishings

living room	refrigerator	shelf — shelves
dining room	balcony	sofa
kitchen	dresser	table lamp
armchair	closet	desk lamp
coffee table	washroom	desk
night table	bathroom	master bedroom
sink	cupboard	bedroom
stove	bookcase	

Useful expressions

on each side	to the right/left of	below
beside	near	in front of
on the table	above	behind
in the corner	over	square
on the floor	opposite	round
off the master bedroom	under	rectangular
against the wall	by	
between	next to	

Here is a floor plan of an apartment.
With the help of the teacher, you will describe this apartment.

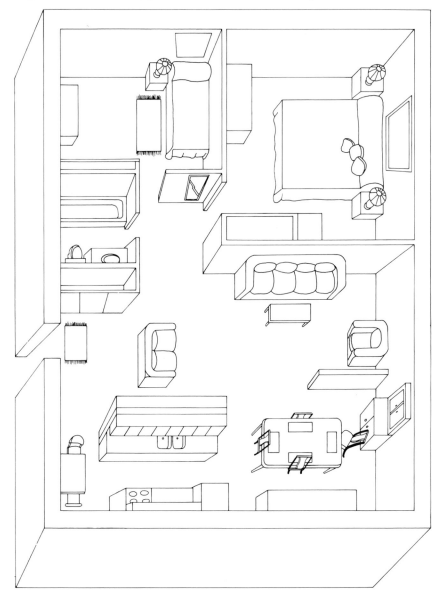

Activity 7. Furnishing is Fun

Draw furniture and lots of other items you want on the room plan you have been given. Do not let your partner see your drawings.

Then describe your plan to your partner. He/she will try to draw what you say. See if he/she can draw the same floor plan as you have drawn from your description alone. After you have finished, switch roles. Your partner will now try to describe his/her room and you will try to draw it. At the end your rooms should be the same as your partner's rooms.

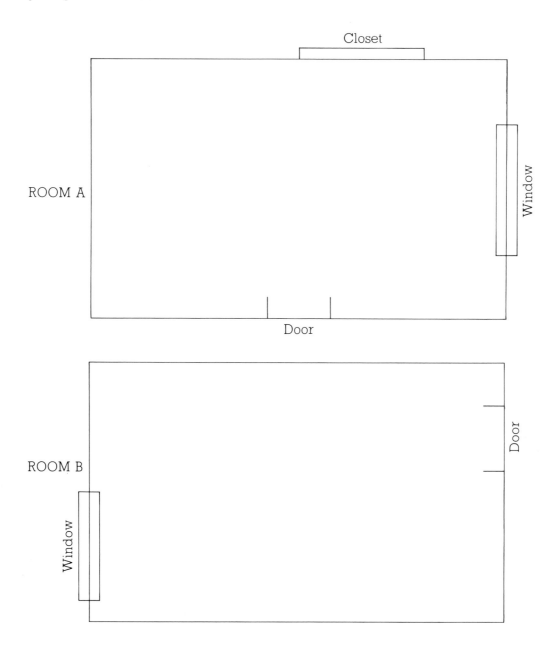

Activity 8. Map Directions

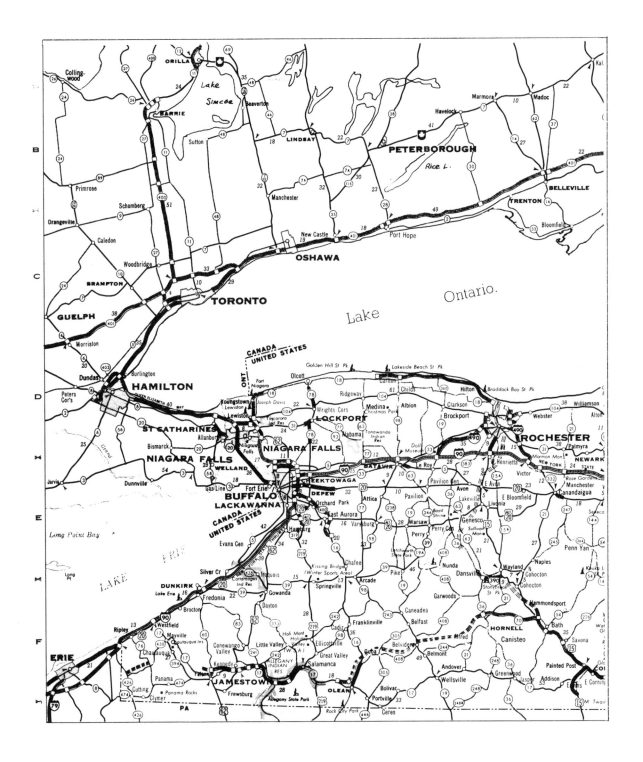

Here are some expressions we use when we're giving directions using a road map:

Drive north on I-90 (Interstate-90).

Take Highway 400 north.

Exit at Highway 31A.

Just past Buffalo.

Continue on Highway 11.

Drive for about/approximately 21 km. (13 miles).

Make a left onto Highway 23.

Remember: we often use the imperative form to give directions.
  (e.g. *turn* left, *go* straight, etc.)

Now the teacher will give you some directions. See if you can follow the directions.

Activity 9. Pick a Place

This is a game in which you use the road map. You have invited some friends to come and visit you.

1. Choose the town or city you want to "live" in and choose the town or city your friends come from. Do not tell them where you live!

2. Give one friend the directions of how to get to your town: the highways, the directions, in order to get there from their town.

3. Make sure your directions are clear enough for your friend to find your town, using the map.

4. Your friend must write down the name of your town on a piece of paper.

Remember to make your directions clear and to use short sentences.

Now, your friend will read you his/her directions, as you follow along and try to guess where he/she lives.

5. When both of you have done this, find another friend and do the same thing again.

At the end of the class, you will see if your directions were easy to follow by the number of people who correctly guessed where you live.

UNIT III. PART A   INTERRUPTING

Sometimes when we hear something being said, we want to join the conversation; for example, at work or at a party. If we are already in a group and want to add another point to what is being said, we use certain polite expressions.

Look at the following list of expressions:

Pardon me for interrupting, but (I think) . . .
Excuse me for interrupting, but . . .
May/could I say something here?
If I might/may/could come in here?
If I might/may/could come in again?
I'd like to say something about that (if I may).
May I ask a question?

When you have been interrupted by someone, there are certain other expressions which will help you get back to the original topic. These are:

Getting back to . . .
Going back to . . .
As I was saying (before) . . .
Where was I?

Or you may want the speaker, who has been interrupted by another person, to get back to the original topic. You could then use some of the expressions below:

Please go on.
Please continue.
As you were saying . . .

In most conversations, you will find the above expressions quite useful. You will practice them and see how they work.

Work in groups of three. Two of you will hold a conversation on a topic of your choice, and the third person will interrupt.

UNIT III. PART B EXPRESSING LIKES AND DISLIKES

Sample Dialogs

The following are some dialogs expressing likes and dislikes. You will find these useful when working on the various activities in this Unit.

1. *STRONG LIKE:*

    Antonio: There's a new play opening tonight. I'd like to go.
                How about you?
     Jerry: *Great!* What time can you pick me up?

2. *WEAK LIKE:*

     Mickey: How was the movie last night?
   Danielle: It was *all right.*

3. *STRONG DISLIKE:*

     Abdul: I'm going for a pizza. Want to come?
   Susan : I *hate* pizza! How can you eat such *awful* stuff?

4. *WEAK DISLIKE:*

  Alexandra: How about a movie tonight?
      Lisa: I *don't really feel* like it.
  Alexandra: ''2001'' is playing!
      Lisa: I'm *not mad about* science fiction.

Here are some key words and expressions:

STRONG LIKE

I love . . .
I adore . . .
I really like . . .
Great!
Terrific!
Super!
Marvelous!
Wonderful!

WEAK LIKE

I like . . .
It's all right.
It's okay.
Nice.
Not bad.

STRONG DISLIKE

I hate . . .
I detest . . .
I can't stand . . .
Forget it!
Not at all!
Not my type of thing!
Awful!
Terrible!
Dreadful!
Yuk!

WEAK DISLIKE

I'm not mad/crazy about . . .
I'm not very fond of . . .
I don't like . . .
I dislike . . .
I don't (particularly) care for . . .
It'll do.
Not much.
Not particularly.

Activity 1. Classifying Responses

When a suggestion is made or a question is asked, we often want to respond to it and in this way say how we feel.

A. In the following exercise, we will look at a few such short exchanges.

1. Do you like New York?   Very much. It's so cosmopolitan.
2. Do you like hockey?   I think it's a terrific sport.
3. Do you like Anne?   She's a nice person.
4. Do you like watermelon?   Delicious!
5. Do you like maple sugar?   Delicious, but a bit too sweet.
6. Would you like a beer?   Uh . . . only if there's nothing else.
7. What did you think of his report?   It'll do.
8. Do you like compact cars?   They're okay for city driving.
9. Do you like hamburgers?   Not much.
10. What do you think of
Canadian winters?   Terrible!

Which of the expressions used in the responses are expressions of strong like, weak like, strong dislike, and weak dislike?
How did you decide?

B. Now, working in groups of three, use the same questions and try to think of different yet appropriate answers to these questions.

(a) The first person will ask the next person a question; the second person will reply, using his/her own answer.

(b) The third person will decide whether the second person's answer was an expression of like or dislike, and if it was a strong or weak expression.

(c) Then continue; this time the second person asks the question, and so on.

Activity 2. Do you like . . . ?

Look at the following expressions: It's not bad.
It's so-so.
I prefer X to Y.

Here are two sample dialogs:

Helmut: What do you think of cola drinks?
  Denis: They're not bad.

  Linda: Do you like cola drinks?
  Sacha: I prefer orange drinks.

Now, work in pairs. Find out what your partner thinks about various things:

snakes	outdoor cafés
avocados	science fiction
the color blue	studying English
Shakespeare	discotheques
housework	jogging

plus two items of your own choice

Activity 3.   What Class Activities do You Like?

1. Each of you will list five possible activities that you would like to do as a class. Then we will discuss these activities in the class, and you will express your like or dislike of the various activities suggested. We will then choose the most popular activities.

2. Now we will talk about different areas of life. Some suggested topics:
    1. A country you would like to live in.
    2. Chinese/French/American restaurants.
    3. Co-educational/private/public schools.
    4. European/North American/other films.
    5. City/country.
    6. Private homes/apartments.
    7. Qualities in a husband/wife.
    8. Old age homes/the aged living at home.

Activity 4.   Planning a Night Out

You and your partner(s) are going to make plans for a night out. Use a page from the newspaper that shows what's happening at the theater, movies, galleries and in sports. State your likes and dislikes. Remember to use as many different expressions as you can, both strong and weak forms. Try to reach agreement. If necessary, refer to the dialogs and expressions at the beginning of this Unit.

After you finish the discussion, one person from your group will report to the class as follows:

(a) The suggestions made.
(b) Who liked/disliked what, and how strongly/weakly that person felt about the suggestion.
(c) The student reporting should be able to give the other student's exact words so that the class can decide that this was a strong/weak expression of like/dislike.

Activity 5. Taking a Poll

In this game you have about ten minutes. You are going to find out each person's strongest like and dislike.

You should try to approach as many students as possible in the time you are allowed. When you are asked about your likes/dislikes, you should answer using different expressions of strong like or dislike:

Example: The first time you are approached about food, you might answer: "*I adore shrimp and I detest broiled fish.*"

The second time, when asked about music, you should not use *adore, detest,* but say: "*I'm extremely fond of rock music but I can't stand folk music.*"

Use the following chart and work as fast as you can:

NAME	STRONG LIKE	STRONG DISLIKE
1.		
2.		
3.		
4.		
5.		
6.		
7.		
8.		
9.		
10.		
11.		
12.		
13.		
14.		
15.		
16.		
17.		
18.		
19.		
20.		

Activity 6. Being Tactful

A. Sometimes we have to be polite about something or someone even though we do not really like them. This is called "being tactful."

   The following is a dialog in which Sandy is being tactful:

   Lee: How do you like my new sweater?

   Sandy: It's an interesting color.

   Lee: And what about the style? Isn't it just terrific?

   Sandy: Yeah.

   Lee: And the wool — it's so soft. Wasn't this a good buy?

   Sandy: Certainly was.

   Now answer the following questions:

   1. Does Lee like her new purchase?
   2. Does Sandy like Lee's new purchase?
   3. How and why is Sandy being tactful?

B. We are frequently expected to be tactful when expressing dislikes.
   What do you think are some of the reasons for this?
   Working in small groups, think of some situations where you might have to be polite or tactful. Then plan a short dialog based on one situation. If necessary, refer back to the key words and expressions at the beginning of the Unit.

   Think about whether this is different in your culture.

C. *A Game*

   You are invited to dinner at an English-speaking friend's house.
   During dinner you are asked the following questions by the father:

   1. How are you enjoying your stay in this city?
   2. How do you find the food here?
   3. What about the weather? Must be different from your country's.
   4. And what do you think of your English classes?

   Actually, you strongly dislike all the things you are asked about.

Working in groups, think of some tactful answers. Remember that you *must* keep the conversation going because you are there for the whole evening, and you must not offend anyone by being tactless.

Activity 7.   Learning Strong and Weak Expressions

Read these pairs of dialogs. In all of them the person answering is saying whether he/she liked or disliked something. Then answer and discuss the questions.

Mr. Jones and Mr. Robinson are answering their bosses' questions, so they have to be polite.

A. Mr. Lovatt (the boss): What did you think of Mr. Silk's report at the meeting?

   Mr. Jones (his employee): I thought it was extremely clear and very well thought out! He worked so hard on it!

B. Mr. Flavell (the boss): What did you think of Ms. Love's report at the meeting?

   Mr. Robinson (his employee): I found it good and clear.

(a) In Dialog A, did Mr. Jones like Mr. Silk's report?

(b) In Dialog B, did Mr. Robinson like Ms. Love's report?

(c) How did you decide your answers to (a) and (b)?

(d) Who was more pleased with the report: Mr. Jones in (a) or Mr. Robinson in (b)?

(e) How did you decide your answer to (d)?

*   *   *

C.   Paul (husband): Do you want to go to a concert tomorrow night?
        Linda (wife): I'd prefer to go to a play.

D.   Bernice (wife): Do you want to go to that lecture tomorrow night?
    Frank (husband): Forget it! I can't stand lectures!

In Dialog C Linda didn't like Paul's idea, and in Dialog D Frank didn't like Bernice's idea.

(f) How do you know?

(g) Did Linda dislike Paul's idea very much, or did she not show very strong dislike?

(h) How did you decide your answer to (g)?

(i) Did Frank dislike Bernice's idea very much, or did he not show very strong dislike?

(j) How did you decide your answer to (i)?

(k) Frank used the expression "forget it" to express strong dislike of an idea to his wife. Do you think he would use this expression to his boss, and why?

*   *   *

In the next two dialogs, E and F, the people are friends.

E. Mary-Anne: Did you enjoy "Opera on Ice" on T.V.?

        Janice: Not at all. Not my type of thing.

F.   Bruce: Did you enjoy that new T.V. program about opera?
        Bernie: Not particularly. But then I'm not mad about classical music.

Janice (in E) and Bernie (in F) are expressing dislikes.

   (l)   Whose dislike is stronger: Janice's or Bernie's?

   (m) How did you decide your answer to (l)?

Activity 8.   The Disco Lesson

The setting: All the people in all the dialogs were at *the same party* given by Vince and Caroline. At the party, there was a dancing teacher whom Vince had paid to teach disco dancing.

Group Work: Read each dialog and answer these four questions, after discussing them in the group:

(a) Did the person answering like or dislike the idea of teaching disco dancing at the party?

(b) Discuss how you decided your answer to (a).

(c) Was the like/dislike strong or weak?

(d) Discuss how you decided on your answer to (c).

Notice the relationship between the two people holding the conversation. Sometimes the dialog is more formal because of the relationship, or more informal for the same reason.

Dialogs

A.   Mr. Brown (the boss): How did you like Vince's idea of having a disco
                               lesson at the party?
     Mr. Martin (his employee): I thought it was a very nice idea.
                               He really thought about it before he decided on this.

                        *   *   *

B. Arthur (husband): How did you like the idea of the disco lesson?
        Faith (wife): Super! Just a great idea!

                        *   *   *

C.   Mr. Brown (the boss): How did you like Vince's idea of having a disco
                               lesson at the party?
     Ms. White (his employee): I thought it was nice.

                        *   *   *

D. Denise (close friend): How did you like Vince's idea of having a disco lesson
                            at the party?
        Paul (close friend): Nice.

                        *   *   *

E. Mr. Brown (the boss): How did you like Vince's idea of having a disco lesson at the party?

Veronica Simmons (his employee): To be honest, I thought it was not at all suitable. It was a very poor idea.

* * *

F. Fred (close friend): How did you like the idea of the disco lesson?

Lois (close friend): Dreadful! What got into the guy!

* * *

G. Mr. Brown (the boss): How did you like Vince's idea of having a disco lesson at the party?

Lionel Gormsley (his employee): It certainly was original.

* * *

H. Brian (husband): How did you like the idea of the disco lesson?

Lois (wife): Not particularly. A bit silly.

Activity 9. Do I Like It?

You work in pairs. Student A chooses one of the situations. Then you develop a dialog in which Student A asks Student B a question based on the situation.

Example: *A friend asks a friend about a trip to Paris.*

Student A asks: *How did you enjoy your trip to Paris?*

(Student B must decide whether to answer expressing LIKE or DISLIKE, in a STRONG or WEAK way). So, if Student B decides to answer expressing, say, strong like, he/she would answer:

Student B: *Fantastic! What a great city!*

After you present your dialog to the class, Student B asks the class:

1. Did I enjoy the trip?
2. Was this a strong expression or a weak expression?

SEE HOW SUCCESSFULLY YOU CAN COMMUNICATE:

Situations

1. A wife asks a husband about a new dress she's bought.
2. A friend ask a friend about a movie.
3. A boss asks an employee about the new secretary.
4. A parent asks a child about a new type of breakfast cereal.
5. A stranger asks a visitor whether he/she likes Canada.
6. A teacher asks a student about studying computers.
7. A student asks a student about a new teacher.
8. A secretary asks a secretary about a new typewriter.

9. A friend asks a friend about orange juice.
10. A boss asks a secretary about working four days a week, but longer hours.
11. A mother asks a daughter about mother's new hair style.
12. An uncle/aunt asks a niece/nephew about summer camp.
13. A boss asks an employee about his/her new job.
14. A friend asks a friend about his/her new job.
15. An uncle/aunt asks a cousin about a university course.
16. A friend asks a friend about a new building in the city.
17. A sister asks a brother about her cooking.
18. A salesperson asks a customer about an item he/she's been looking at.
19. A doctor asks a patient about the wallpaper in the waiting room.
20. A friend asks a friend about a T.V. program.
21. A friend asks a friend about a party they went to.
22. A waiter asks the guest how he/she liked the dinner.
23. A friend asks a friend about a new car.
24. A son/daughter asks a parent about the new stereo system.
25. A parent asks a babysitter how he/she liked looking after the baby.

UNIT IV. MAKING SUGGESTIONS

Activity 1. Learning to Make Direct Suggestions

The following dialogs have examples of *direct* suggestions.

1. Patient: But doctor, I dislike taking medicine.
   Doctor: Mrs. Rodriques, you suffer from high blood pressure because you are overweight. I suggest that you lose weight, and you won't need to take medicine.

2. John: James, I'm really worried about you. You always have such a bad cough.
   James: It's because I smoke.
   John: Well, you'd better quit smoking.

Now look at this third dialog, in which Mari makes a suggestion to Betty, but she is not being direct — she is being very careful and *tactful.*

The situation:

Betty and Mari, who are friends, live in the same apartment building. Mari's apartment is directly below Betty's, and Betty's children often make a terrible noise playing with a ball in their room, and this disturbs Mari. When Betty talks about her children, Mari takes the opportunity of making a tactful suggestion that they make their noise somewhere else.

3. Betty: My kids are driving me crazy. They fight and scream a lot and really bug each other.
   Mari: Why don't you arrange for them to join a sports club?
   My kids get rid of a lot of their energy that way.

Here are some useful expressions for making *direct* suggestions:

I suggest (you) . . .	You had better . . .
Try . . .	You'd better . . .
I would . . .	You could . . .
I'd . . .	I suggest that you . . .

Now you try to make direct suggestions in little dialogs. Choose one of the situations, and don't tell anyone except your partner, and prepare your dialog. They should be like those in the first two dialogs, and you should use the expressions above. The rest of the class will judge your efforts, using the four questions below:

1. You have a constant headache (see a doctor).
2. You can't wake up in the morning (use an alarm clock).

3. You have a toothache (see a dentist).
4. You are homesick (phone home).
5. You are overweight (lose weight).
6. You smoke (quit smoking).
7. You are out of condition (start jogging).
8. You need a rest (take a holiday).
9. You need some clothes (go shopping).
10. Your bicycle was stolen (buy a new one).
11. You are always tired in class (go to bed earlier).
12. Your typing is full of mistakes (be more careful).

While listening to the different dialogs, the rest of the class should think about these questions, and then discuss them afterwards:

1. Who was speaking to whom?
2. What was the relationship between the speakers?
3. Was the suggestion *direct*?
4. If it was direct, was that appropriate and why?

Activity 2. The Teacher's Dilemma

In the two situations that the teacher will describe to you, she really needs your help. Because she is asking for your help, you should make *direct* suggestions using the expressions you've learned.

As suggestions are being made, you should fill them in on the charts.

Situation 1: What Should We do in Class Tomorrow?

Suggestion Chart

1.

2.

3.

4.

5.

Situation 2:   How do I Tell Kim?

Suggestion Chart

1.

2.

3.

4.

5.

Activity 3.   Let's Discuss Juan's Dilemma

Juan has a problem. He wants to get married to Anne, a nice English-speaking girl he has met. Juan and his mother are new to the country and at the moment he is living with his mother. His mother is in good health and has a lot of money. After Juan gets married, he wants his mother to live with them. However, Anne doesn't like Juan's mother and doesn't want her to live with them. She says Juan's mother has her own house and she can live there by herself. Now Juan doesn't know what to do. He loves Anne and his mother.

Try to think of as many suggestions as possible to help them solve their problem.

Activity 4.   Learning to Make Tactful Suggestions

There are occasions when you have to be very careful when making a suggestion. You don't want to insult or offend the person. When this is the situation, we use "softer" ways of making a suggestion — we are more tactful, and less direct. Here are some expressions to use when you want to make a tactful suggestion:

Why don't you . . .

Do you think . . .

Don't you think it might be a good idea to . . .

Why not . . .

We could always . . .

Perhaps you could . . .

One way would/could be to . . .

Why don't we . . .

Perhaps we could . . .

You really should . . .

Look at these two dialogs which have tactful suggestions:

Dialog A

Bob: I'm very upset. My boss, Ms. Lewiston, is being unkind and unfriendly to me.

Tak (his friend): Don't you think it might be a good idea to talk to her about it?

Dialog B

Mr. Haycraft (at the bank): Again, your bank has made a mistake with my account. I'm really very angry. I think I'm going to move to another bank.

Mr. Yuen (the bank manager): Why don't you come into my office and talk. Perhaps we could look at this together.

Now you will be given a problem to solve. Prepare your tactful suggestion. Afterwards, you will read your problem to the class, hear what they suggest, and then tell them what suggestion you made.

1. I don't know what to do at night because my roommate snores. What do you suggest I say to him/her?
2. I haven't received mail from home for three weeks. What should I do?
3. My father dislikes my boyfriend/girlfriend. What can I do?
4. What is a good souvenir to take home to my girlfriend/boyfriend? Any suggestions? (Be careful because the speaker is short of money.)
5. Someone has invited me to dinner, but I don't like him. What can I do?
6. I won a million dollars. What do you suggest I do with the money?
7. I have received many bills for my cousin who has a similar name. What should I say to him/her?
8. There is a cute boy/girl in the other class. How can I meet him/her?
9. My tooth hurts and my dentist says there's nothing wrong. Help!
10. I've been invited to a masquerade party. What can I wear to it? I'm so fat!
11. Some new friends have invited me to dinner. I don't take anything, do I?
12. I am bored and have nothing to do on weekends. Give me some suggestions. (Be careful because the speaker is short of money.)
13. My boyfriend doesn't know how to cook. What am I to say to him?
14. I want to lose weight. Help me!
15. My boss gives me too much work. What should I do?
16. My teacher has invited me to a movie. I don't want to go. What can I do?
17. My doctor doesn't understand my English, so I want to change doctors. What should I do?
18. A student in my class keeps calling me. My husband/wife is getting angry. What should I do?

Activity 5.   Talking to Juan about his Problem

In Activity 3 we discussed solutions to Juan's problem. Juan was not here, so we were able to talk quite directly about his problem. This time, you will be talking to Juan, so your suggestions will have to be much more tactful. You should use expressions you learned in Activity 4. The teacher will take Juan's part. Remember: your job is to help Juan without insulting or offending him.

Activity 6.   Personally Speaking

In this activity you will get more practice in making tactful suggestions. Before you do, look at these expressions which can also be used to tactfully suggest an alternative.

On the other hand . . .	Still . . .
That's very true but . . .	Nevertheless . . .
However . . .	Instead . . .

Now look at an example of how these can be used in conversation:

Lucille: I'm very angry with Fred. He forgot my birthday. When his birthday comes, I'm going to forget his!

Vera: On the other hand, if you told him nicely, I'm sure you would both be happier.

Lucille: You're right. We all forget things, I suppose. I'll mention my birthday this evening, and let you know what happens.

The teacher will now give you a task to prepare for the next class, using what we've been learning.

Activity 7.   Mo's Your Friend

If you dial 749-0202, you will get Mo on the line. Mo will talk to anyone who calls with a problem. This service is called "Mo's your friend," and whenever you call 749-0202, Mo answers: "Hello, Mo's your friend."

Look at this conversation that took place a few weeks ago when a caller called Mo:

Caller: (dials 749-0202): Hello.

Mo: Hello, Mo's your friend.

Caller: Hi Mo, I have a big problem.

Mo: Why don't you tell me about it. I'm sure between us we can think of a solution.

Caller: Well, the problem is my mother-in-law. You see, she lives in an apartment in the same city as we do, and we help her financially every month.

Mo: Uh-huh.

Caller: Well, on weekends, sometimes I lend her my car, but she's ruining it. Now I want to buy a new car, but I don't want her to ruin it. What can I do?

Mo: Why not offer to give her some lessons, because it's a new car?

Caller: She'd be very insulted. She thinks she's a terrific driver.

Mo: Okay. Don't you think it might be a good idea then to talk to her about it?

Caller: No way! It would only cause a huge fight.

Mo: I have a better idea. Why not give her the old car when you buy the new one. You say it's ruined anyway.

Caller: I think you're right. It's only worth $1500.00 and I think that would be an excellent solution. Thanks a lot, Mo, for your suggestions.

Mo: You're welcome. Bye now.

Caller: Goodbye

Now, in pairs, plan a ''Mo's your friend'' dialog like this one.

UNIT V. MAKING SMALL TALK

Activity 1. What is Small Talk?

In this activity we are going to learn to recognize and use small talk.

Together with the class, answer the following questions to find out what small talk is.

1. Have you ever been in a situation where you want to say something to someone and don't know what to say or how to start?
2. What do you think can be said in a situation like that to start a conversation?
3. Where is small talk used?
4. Who uses small talk?
5. Whom do we make small talk with?
6. Why is it important to be able to make small talk?
7. In what kinds of situations do we use small talk, and why?

Now read the following dialog. Be ready to talk about it with the class.

Kim: It's hot in here, isn't it?

Jill: Yes, it certainly is. I wish they'd open a window or two.

Kim: That would be nice. By the way, my name is Kim.

Jill: Hi, I'm Jill.

Kim: Do you take classes here?

Jill: Yes, I'm in English 101. What class are you in?

Kim: English 201.

Jill: Is it an interesting class?

Kim: It's okay.

Jill: Is it easy to get here from where you live?

Kim: Yes, it takes me 45 minutes by bus. How long does it take you to get to school?

Jill: About the same. I have to rush. I'm going to be late for class. Nice meeting you.

Kim: Bye now.

Activity 2.   What Small Talk Is NOT

In the following dialogs you will read some examples of what is not acceptable as small talk in English. See if you can guess why not.

The first speaker is an English speaker from North America. The second speaker is from an imaginary country. They are strangers, meeting at a party for the first time.

1.   Peter: I've got a nice job in the city.
     Ulu: How much do you make?
2.   Jon: I'm a student at the university.
     Ogo: How old are you?
3. Gabriel: I've just visited Litas and had a lovely time there.
     Hindi: I heard there's a communist government there.
4.   Marian: Do you like the new ring my husband gave me?
     Buto: Yes. How much did it cost?
5.   Sue: Hello, I'm Annie's cousin.
     Jesta: You drink a lot, don't you?
6.   Di: My office was really hot today.
     Wun: Boy, do you need a shower!

A. Discuss with your teacher why people living here would find the above dialogs rude.
B. Since the second speaker's comments are unsuitable, change them to more appropriate answers.

Activity 3.   What CAN I Talk About?

In the last activity you saw that there are some things that we prefer not to talk about when first meeting someone. Yet there are many topics we can and do talk about. Let's discuss some of these.

Impersonal topics:

1. the weather: yesterday's, tomorrow's, today's
2. inflation: the price of everyday things like coffee, newspapers, clothes
3. travel: problems encountered at airports, subways, customs, taxi stands
4. news: local, national, world (be careful to pick a neutral topic like earthquakes, discoveries, etc.)
5. entertainment: movies, concerts, theaters, dances, T.V., radio, music
6. sports: hockey, football, soccer
7. tourist attractions: Niagara Falls, the Statute of Liberty
8. your surroundings: office, house, furniture

Personal topics:

We sometimes also use personal topics for small talk. We do this out of politeness, but we should be very careful not to try to get details. All we want to do is to make conversation.

1. health: yours, your family's
2. job: hours, place, type of work
3. family: wife, husband, children, pets
4. friends: health, jobs
5. hobbies and weekend activities

* * *

Here are two sample dialogs:

An example of a dialog using an impersonal topic:

    David: I think it's going to rain.

Marianne: Well, I don't mind. They said on the radio it'll be clear tomorrow.

    David: I don't know. I think it'll rain all day tomorrow too.

Marianne: Oh, that's awful. I want to go to the beach tomorrow.

* * *

An example of a dialog using a personal topic:

    Joan: How's David?

Maureen: He's not feeling well.

    Joan: Oh, what's wrong?

Maureen: He's got the flu.

    Joan: That's too bad. I hope he soon gets better.

Maureen: Thanks. I'll tell him.

Activity 4. Getting the Other Person to Make Small Talk

One way of getting people to talk is by asking them questions on one of the small talk topics. Besides asking regular questions such as "Is it going to rain tomorrow?," you can use two other types of questions: wh-questions and tag questions to get people to make small talk.

Some examples of the type of wh-questions you can use:

how	How did you get here tonight in all that rain?
when	When did you come to this country?
what	What are your plans for the future?
where	Where are you studying?
why	Why did you come to John Black College?

Some examples of tag questions:

isn't it	This is your first visit here, isn't it?
haven't they	They have a lovely home, haven't they?
hasn't it	It's been hot lately, hasn't it?

Or you can ask them their opinion of something:

What do you think of X?

Do you like X?

*   *   *

Now it is your turn to practice. With a partner, choose two or three topics from Activity 3 and try making small talk with him or her.

Try to use each type of question at least once.

Activity 5. You Be Alex

In the following dialog, as a class you will try to guess what Alex would say.

In a crowded doctor's waiting room on a hot summer's day:

Cathie: Boy, it certainly is hot in here.
  Alex:

Cathie: Do you know if this terrible weather will continue?
  Alex:

Cathie: It happens every year. You'd think people would be ready for it, especially in a place like this.
  Alex:

Cathie: Air conditioning certainly would be nice right now.
  Alex:

Cathie: Gee, it's 2:30 already. What time is your appointment?
  Alex:

Cathie: Oh, mine was at 2. Do you think we'll have to wait much longer?
  Alex:

Cathie: Oh . . . I hear my name being called. Nice talking to you.
  Alex:

With a partner, choose one of the following dialogs and fill it in. Be ready to act out your dialog.

1. Waiting for an elevator:

  Brian: This elevator is certainly taking a long time.
    Leo:

  Brian: I've been here for at least five minutes.
    Leo:

  Brian: I wonder if it got stuck?
    Leo:

  Brian: Or maybe it's broken.
    Leo:

40

Brian: I'd hate to be stuck in an elevator.
  Leo:
Brian: Oh, really. It must have been frightening.
  Leo:
Brian: Finally. Here it comes. Guess it's working all right after all.

2. Bernard and Greta have just met for the first time at a friend's apartment during a party. Try to guess what Greta is saying:

Bernard: Oh, . . . I can see that you like flowers.
  Greta:
Bernard: What else do you like besides flowers?
  Greta:
Bernard: Do you? What have you read lately?
  Greta:
Bernard: Oh, . . . they, they must be like a kind of drug, uh, very addictive.
  Greta:
Bernard: I should read one some day.
  Greta:
Bernard: It might be interesting.
  Greta:
Bernard: Yeah, I may learn something new.
  Greta:
Bernard: Yeah, I play tennis.
  Greta:
Bernard: Oh, a couple of times a week.
  Greta:
Bernard: Yeah, especially after you've been playing it for five years.
  Greta:
Bernard: Well, you'll have to excuse me now . . . I want to grab something to eat.
  Greta:

Activity 6. Ending a Conversation

In English we do not suddenly say goodbye. Instead we first of all signal that we are about to finish and only then do we say goodbye.

Look at the following examples:

1. Anna: It was nice talking to you.
  Scott: My pleasure.
  Anna: Goodbye.
2. Bob: I enjoyed talking to you.
  Alan: Thank you.
  Bob: Bye.

3. Sue: I have to go now.
    Steve: Right.
    Sue: So long.
4. Anne: Well, I'll let you go now.
    Sami: O.K.
    Anne: Be seeing you.

NOTE: "Bye-bye" is often used when talking to children and may be used for adults.

Here are some more closings:

Sorry, but I've got to run.
Sorry to rush off, but I have to be going.
Sorry, but I must go.

Now, try making a few ending dialogs with your partner. Be sure that they are natural sounding.

Activity 7. Creating Small Talk

Now it is your turn. Working in pairs, create a dialog illustrating small talk. You should base your dialog on one of the sets of information listed below. Be ready to show it to the class. The class will then evaluate it. You may find you will have to change your dialog after the class evaluates it to make it more acceptable as small talk.

Some sets of information to build your dialogs:

1. In the cafeteria at lunch time; two students from different classes sit beside each other and they are strangers.
2. In the doctor's waiting room; a man with a cast on his arm and a woman with a broken leg also in a cast.
3. In line at the airline counter; the line is moving slowly.
4. In line for a popular movie; it is starting to rain.
5. In a lawyer's office; the only other person in the waiting room is a very attractive person you would like to meet.

Checklist:

As you are listening to the other students present their dialogs, use this checklist to help you evaluate them.

	Yes	Could be better	No
1. Was the dialog too formal?			
2. Were the topics appropriate?			
3. Did the dialog sound natural?			
4. Was it, as small talk, successful?			

Any other comments or suggestions:

UNIT VI — AGREEING AND DISAGREEING

Words and Expressions for Agreeing Strongly

There are various ways of agreeing and disagreeing. It is possible to agree in a strong or weak manner; and it is possible to disagree in a strong or weak manner.

Here are some words and expressions for *agreeing strongly*:

Absolutely.	I agree entirely.
Certainly.	I agree 100%.
Definitely.	I couldn't agree with you more.
Sure.	That's just what I think.
It's true.	That's exactly what I was thinking.
No doubt about it.	I agree with you completely.
Sounds good.	You know, that's exactly what I think.
Sounds great.	
Right.	
I'd love to.	
And how.	

Activity 1. Learning to Express Strong Agreement

There are many ways of expressing strong agreement. Here is a dialog using some of the above expressions.

Note that in this dialog reasons are given for agreeing.

Sample Dialog 1

Janine: I always get angry when I hear that an old person was robbed.

Jim: Me too. Imagine attacking someone who can't defend himself! It's shameful!

Janine: Absolutely! They should be in jail.

Jim: I couldn't agree with you more!

Another way of agreeing is simply just to use one of the above expressions *without* an explanation. The following dialog shows us this.

Sample Dialog 2

Jorge: This place is wonderful, isn't it?

Betty: Sure is!

Jorge: Lovely trees, flowers and avenues.

Betty: Absolutely!

Jorge: Terrific restaurants with good food.
 Betty: And how!
Jorge: And the nightlife is just fantastic.
 Betty: No doubt about it!

Working in threes, each of you pick a topic and practice agreeing *strongly* with the opinion of one of your partners (even though you may disagree in real life with it). The third person will be an observer.

1. First try it without an explanation.
2. Then try it with an explanation.

        Some suggested topics:

        Advertising
        Smoking
        Old age homes
        Modern music
        Sports on television
        Television
        Nuclear energy
        Jogging
        North American food
        Any subject of your choice

Activity 2. Don't you Agree?

Take turns in agreeing with the following statements. Don't give any reason. Just use a strong expression of agreement.

Nice day, isn't it?
Good lunch, wasn't it?
She has a pretty dress on.
I hate curry in my food.
May looks tired.
What a beautiful view!
It looks like rain.
It's really hot in here.
Great meal.

Now, each of you make up a few of your own comments like the ones above and have someone agree with them, using a different expression each time.

Activity 3. Learning to Express Weak Agreement

Sometimes we agree but not so strongly. There are other times when we have to agree as we have no choice. When this is the case, we use expressions that show weak agreement. The following expressions and dialogs are examples of this.

Expressions:

I don't mind.
I suppose so.
If you have to.
If you must.
Okay.

Dialogs:

1.   Jaime: Where'll we go for lunch? How about the coffee shop?
       Bill: *I don't mind.*

2.   Lee: I need some help with this lesson. Could you help me after class today?
       Jane: *I suppose so.*

3.   Howard (the boss): How about a cup of coffee before going home?
       Jacques (an employee): Uh . . . *Okay.*

After you have practiced these dialogs, make up some situations of your own.

Activity 4. Sure, but . . .

Another way of showing weak agreement is to use an expression of strong agreement, adding words to show that it is weak agreement. Look at how this is done in the following three dialogs, and practice them.

1.   Ann: Good lunch, wasn't it?
     Arnold: Sure, but it was a bit too salty.

2.   Joan: This city is a great place to live.
      Peter: I agree, but only in the summer.

3.   Miriam: Will you come shopping with me?
     Michael: I'd love to, but only for half an hour.

After you practice these, create some situations, and use this form of weak agreement. Some subjects you can use are:

> Movies
> Books
> Pets
> Snakes or other animals
> Cars
> Clothes
> Colors

Activity 5. Learning to Disagree

Look at these expressions we use as the first part of expressing disagreement:

I disagree (with you) . . .
I don't agree with you (that) . . .
I don't think that's right . . .
I think . . . (and then you say the opposite of what was said)

We use the following expressions if we want to ask if someone agrees with us:

What do you think?
Do you agree?
Don't you think so?

These expressions come either when a person is asked if he/she agrees, or if something is said and you want to disagree, even if you haven't been asked.

Usually when we disagree with something in English, it's followed by some reason or explanation of *why* we disagree. Look at this example:

Hau: John wants to buy a motorcycle with the money he's saved. I think that's a good idea.
Terry: I disagree with you because I think they're very dangerous.
Hau: I guess you're right. They are dangerous.

Look at what happens if you don't give an explanation:

Hau: John wants to buy a motorcycle with the money he's saved. I think that's a good idea.
Terry: I disagree with you.

When the conversation ends like that in English, it sounds rude and abrupt. So be careful to disagree *politely* — if you do, very often people will accept it. If you just disagree, people will:

1. think you're rude;
2. probably not accept your opinion easily.

There is one way to disagree *without using* disagreeing expressions and still be polite. Look at the following:

Peter: This is a boring city to live in. There's nothing to do at night.
Ruth: I think there's lots to do. It takes time to learn about all the exciting things happening.

Notice that Ruth said: ''I think . . .'' and then said the opposite of what Peter had said. This has the meaning of: ''I disagree with you, Peter''.

Activity 6.   A Disagreeing Game

Now we're going to play a game. Each one of you must think of a statement that you will make that other people can disagree with.

Examples of the types of statements are:

Men are not as clever as women.
Black is a very good color for bedrooms.
The government is wrong to raise taxes.

Be ready to disagree with *anything* anyone in the class may say even if you really agree with them.

Use the expressions we've been learning, *and always give a reason why you disagree!*

Activity 7.   Do you Agree with My Suggestion?

In this activity, you can choose to agree or disagree, either strongly or weakly. You will be in groups of three or four and you will choose an outing for the whole class. Here are some suggestions, but you are free to suggest anything and to give a reason in support of it.

1. Movie — the class should go to a movie. After the movie, we can discuss it.
2. Dinner at a restaurant — having dinner together is a good social activity.
3. Preparing a dinner together — if we prepare dinner together, we will co-operate in many ways, and practice our English.
4. Museum or Art Gallery — a visit to a museum or art gallery is educational as well as social.
5. Historical places — if we visit a historical place, we also learn something about the country.

You should agree or disagree with the suggestion, giving your reason(s). Afterwards we will compare the choices of the different groups.

Activity 8. Friendly Discussions

This activity is done in groups of three. You should choose one of the topics, and you should prepare to take part in a discussion on this topic in the next lesson.

Censorship: 1. Films that are pornographic should be censored.
2. There should be *no* censorship.
3. Children's television programs should be censored.

Sport and   4. Learning sports at school should not be compulsory.
Education   5. Learning a foreign language at school should be compulsory.
6. Learning a musical instrument or dancing should be compulsory.

The Law: 7. Sixteen is too young to drive a car.
8. Car radios should not be allowed to be played very loudly.
9. All new immigrants should be given six months of language training with full support by the government.
10. A person caught drunk when driving should never be allowed to drive again.

Activity 9. Our Group Agrees That . . .

You are going to discuss a topic that the teacher gives you.

Here are the steps to follow:

1. Think about the topic. (a) Give your opinions.
(b) Give your reactions.
(c) Think about it from every point of view.

2. Put your ideas in two lists: one "for" and one "against" the topic, and one of you will keep notes.

3. Then argue for or against the topic, based on your ideas, and give reasons.

4. You must reach a group decision — either agreeing or disagreeing with the topic.

5. Then the whole class will get together and one person from each group will report what decision the group supported, and why.

UNIT VII DESCRIBING

Activity 1. Learning to Describe Objects

You are going to learn how to describe objects.

For example: If the object to be described is a ruler, we could give the following description:

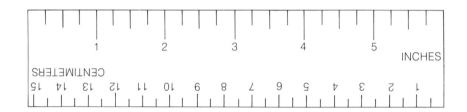

"A ruler is rectangular in shape, and flat. It is usually 15 or 30 cm. (6 or 12 inches) in length, and is made of wood or plastic. Wooden rulers are usually brown, but plastic rulers may be any color. It is used to draw straight lines, and to measure things. Students use rulers in school and when they're doing their homework."

Now let's look at what this description contained:

(1) *Shape* — "A ruler is rectangular in shape and flat."

(2) *Size* — "It is usually 15 or 30 cm. in length."

(3) *What it is made of* — "It is made of wood or plastic."

(4) *Color* — "Wooden rulers are usually brown, but plastic rulers may be any color."

(5) *What it is used for* — "It is used to draw straight lines, and to measure things."

(6) *Where it is found* — "Students use rulers in school, and when they're doing their homework."

There are some very important words or expressions that you need to know when you're describing an object:

1 — Shape

   We can say: It is rectangular in shape.

                 It is shaped like a rectangle.

                 It is shaped like a . . .

                      For example: A television set is shaped like a box.

2 — Size

It is not helpful to say that the object is "big" or "small" because that depends upon what you are comparing it with.

So try to give approximate measurements:

Look, for example, at this box:

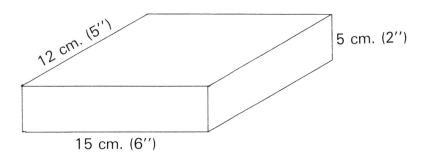

12 cm. (5")   5 cm. (2")

15 cm. (6")

We can say:	It is 15 cm. long.	(It is 6 inches long.)
	It is 15 cm. in length.	(It is 6 inches in length.)
	It is 12 cm. wide.	(It is 5 inches wide.)
	It is 12 cm. in width.	(It is 5 inches in width.)
	It is 5 cm. high.	(It is 2 inches high.)
	It is 5 cm. in height.	(It is 2 inches in height.)

3 — What it is made of

We can say: A box is made of wood.

4 — Color

We can say: It is red.
The color of the box is red.
Its color is red.

5 — What it is used for

We can say: A ruler is used to measure things.
A ruler is used for measuring things.
We use a ruler to measure things.

6 — Where it is found

We can say: It is found (mainly) in schools and offices.
You find it in schools.
It is used (mainly) in schools.

NOTE: Descriptions are usually given in the simple present tense.

e.g. Cars *are* made of metal. We *use* a scale to weigh things.

Now you are going to describe the different objects in these pictures following the method used to describe the ruler:

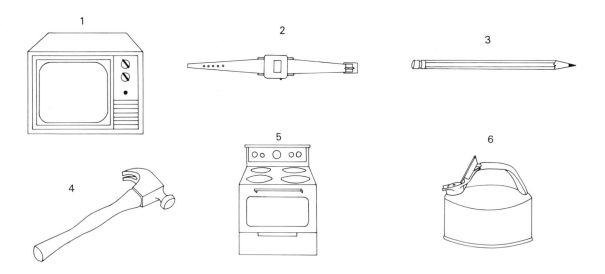

Activity 2. Guess What It Is!

In this activity, you will prepare a description of an object, and then you will present it to the group. After your description, the group will try to guess what the object is.

Do not say what it's made of, or what it's used for. This would make it too easy.

First look at the examples.

Example 1

This object is rectangular in shape. It is about 90 cm. (36 inches) long and 60 cm. (24 inches) wide. It is made of glass and is transparent.

CAN YOU GUESS WHAT IT IS?

If you can't, here's more information: It is found in nearly every room and you look through it.

NOW GUESS WHAT IT IS!

Example 2

This object is usually rectangular in shape. It is about 5 cm. long (2 inches) and 2 cm. ($^3/_4$ inch) wide. It is usually pink or white and is made of rubber.

CAN YOU GUESS WHAT IT IS?

If you can't, here's more information:

It is used to rub out what has been written, and you find it mainly in schools and in offices.

NOW GUESS WHAT IT IS!

Activity 3. Learning to Describe a Scene

In this activity, you will learn how to describe a scene or a place. When you write about a place, you must give enough details to create a "picture" in words. In order to do this, we give information on:

1. *Location* — Where is this place?
2. *Time* — What time of day/month/year is it?
3. *Details* — What are the most important details?
4. *Action* — What is happening? What are people doing?
5. *Sounds* — What sounds do you imagine you would hear if you were there?

Now look at Picture #1 and at the description of it.

Picture #1.

The description:

"In this picture there is a bridge crossing a small river. There are many trees on both sides of the river. It is late in the day. The sun is setting. A few people are sitting under the trees relaxing. It appears very peaceful and quiet."

Notice how the five things we need to include in a description are present. This description is quite correct, but not very detailed and not very interesting. Let's try and add to it, using more adjectives when we describe, and giving more details.

Now look at Picture #2 and at the description of it.

Picture #2

"This is a picture of an open lot next to a house. On the left hand side, next to the house, there is a garage. On the other side is a large tree with a tree-house in it. All around the yard there is a wooden fence. In the middle, between the garage and the tree with the tree-house, there is grass. There is a child and a little black dog playing on the grass with a ball. The child is dressed in summer clothes and is laughing as he plays."

Which description do you think is better: the one of Picture #1 or the one of Picture #2? Why?

Points to notice:

1. When we describe a scene, it is helpful to start with the most important detail.
2. Start the description at one point and go around. You can describe a picture: top to bottom; right to left; left to right; near to far; far to near. *The important thing is to go in a logical order.*
3. Use the simple present tense for most of the description (e.g. "There is a big tree. The garage is old, etc."), except when there is some action, and that is usually described using the present continuous tense (e.g. "The child is laughing").

Here are some words and expressions to use when describing a scene:

there is/there are	at the front/back
in the center	on the left hand side/right hand side
between/in between	behind
on the right/left	on either side
to the right/left	on the other side
at the top/bottom	

Activity 4. My Hometown

On-going Activity

It's always interesting to find out about other people's hometowns. The types of words you need to describe your hometown are:

population	places of interest
suburbs	places to see
downtown	places of historical importance
size	industry
major intersections	hospitals
government buildings	

Now look at a description of Fraserville.

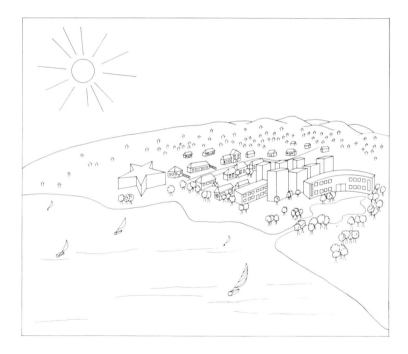

I come from a small town called Fraserville. It's very beautiful, and people always visit our town when they visit our country. It is situated on the shores of Lake Bosco. The population is about 17,000. The suburbs are very modern and clean, and most people live in houses with their own gardens. The town is only 80 years old, so there are not many places of historical importance. But, for a town of its size, there are many beautiful places of interest. The Fraserville Art Gallery is famous because of its collection of paintings by Thomas Bosco Fraser, the famous artist. The town itself is named after Fraser. Fraserville is also the medical center of the whole region, and the Memorial Hospital is a very interesting building. It is shaped like a star to give as much light and sun to the patients as possible. The lake is very popular for summer and winter sports, and . . . well, you should come and see for yourself. I will be your personal guide.

Activity 5.   Same or Different

You will do this activity in pairs. The teacher will give each of you a picture from Set A or from Set B (they are on the following pages). Do not show your partner your picture.

The idea is that one of you will begin by describing one detail in the picture. For example, if we were doing it with Example A and Example B, the person with Example A could say: "In my picture there's a big black cat," and the person with Example B would say: "There's one in my picture also."

You would then go on, detail by detail, building up a complete description and learning how similar/different the two pictures are.

So your discussion would be something like this:

EXAMPLE A   EXAMPLE B

Speaker 1: (looking only at Example A): In my picture there's a big black cat.
Speaker 2: (looking only at Example B): There's one in my picture also. She's sleeping on top of a mailbox.
Speaker 1: Oh no, mine's running across the road.
Speaker 2: In my picture the weather is very hot. People are wearing shorts.
Speaker 1: In mine, it's raining — they all have umbrellas. Any other things in your picture?
Speaker 2: There are two cars in the picture. One is pulling the other.
Speaker 1: Same in mine. That's about all there is in my picture.
Speaker 2: Same with me.

Now you do the same, looking only at the picture that your teacher tells you to look at and describe. If there are any words that you need for your description, ask the teacher.

PICTURE A — 1

PICTURE A — 2

PICTURE A — 3

PICTURE A — 4

56

PICTURE A — 5

PICTURE A — 6

PICTURE A — 7

PICTURE A — 8

PICTURE B — 1

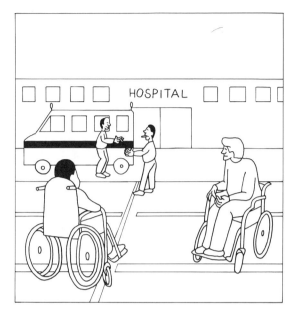

PICTURE B — 2

PICTURE B — 3

PICTURE B — 4

58

PICTURE B — 5

PICTURE B — 6

PICTURE B — 7

PICTURE B — 8

Activity 6. Beautiful Places

Pick a picture from one of the five below, and be ready to describe it to your partner. He/she will try to guess which of the five you are describing, and the two of you should then discuss how good the description was.

You will then listen to your partner's description and do the same.

Here are the five pictures:

A.

B.

C.

D.

E.

Activity 7.   Learning to Describe People

In this activity you are going to learn how to describe people. First, look at these key words and expressions that we use:

He/she is (about) 40 (years old).
tall/short
fat/thin
bald
curly hair/straight hair
He/she is blonde/dark.
He/she wears glasses.
He has a beard/moustache.
He/she looks/seems very . . . (kind, strong, angry, rich, etc.).
smartly dressed/casually dressed
He is (very) handsome.
She is (very) pretty/beautiful/plain.
She has a good figure.

Now read this description.

"I am looking at a picture of a man of about 40. He wears glasses and has a beard. He is dressed casually in a striped shirt and jeans, and he looks like he is thinking. In my opinion he has a very kind face."

Now look at his picture below.

EXAMPLE 1.

1. Do you think this was an accurate description?
2. What do you think he does for a living, and why?

Now look at another description:

"I am now looking at a picture of a woman of about 45. She is wearing a summer dress and scarf, and she has slippers on her feet."

Now look at her picture below.

EXAMPLE 2.

1. Do you think this was an accurate description?
2. What impression do you have of her? What do you think about her? Give reasons.

Now in pairs, you are going to describe one of the people whose picture appears on the next page.

Choose a picture — don't tell your partner which, and don't let your partner open his/her book.

Describe the person in the way the two people were described in the examples, telling:

(a) what you can about what they look like and their age;
(b) what they're wearing.

Try to use the expressions listed on page 60.

Now ask your partner to tell which of the people you were describing.

Discuss with your partner how accurate your description was, what you think the person is doing, what impression you have of the person in the picture and what you think they do for a living.

Then switch and let your partner describe one person to you, and follow this with the same sort of discussion.

Activity 8.   An Emergency

Your friend Wally's wife is having a baby, so he can't go and meet his brother Tom at the airport. He has asked you to go to the airport instead. But you have never met the brother. In a terrible rush (because he has to take his wife to the hospital), he gives you the following description. These are his exact words:

"Tom is tall and dark, wears glasses, and usually dresses formally. I'm sure you'll recognize him. Good luck — I must rush to take Emily to the hospital."

From Wally's description, see if you can guess which one he is in this group photograph.

Now turn over the page and look at a clearer picture of Tom.

TOM

Now you try and give a better description of Tom than Wally did.

Choose another person from the group photograph and describe him/her to your partner. See if your partner can tell which person you are describing. Then switch roles.

Activity 9. Name out of a Hat

The teacher will give you the name of someone in your class. When you receive the name, you will quietly think of how to describe that person.

When you are asked, you will present the description to the whole class. They will try and guess who you are describing.

Be careful not to stare at the person while you are preparing.

Remember: You must describe the person, not what he/she does or where he/she comes from. For example, don't say things like, ''He is a doctor from Venezuela,'' but rather talk about the person's physical features, what he/she is wearing, etc.

UNIT VIII. GIVING OPINIONS

Key Words and Expressions

The following are some key words and expressions used in asking for and giving opinions.

1. *Questions used to get opinions:*
   What do you think?
   What's your opinion?
   How do you feel about . . . ?
   What do you think of/about . . . ?

2. *Expressions for giving opinions:*
   If you ask me . . .
   As I see it, X is . . .
   I think/believe/feel . . .
   In my opinion . . .
   I personally believe/think/feel that . . .
   Personally, I believe/think/feel that . . .
   I'm sure (that) . . .
   I'm positive (that) . . .
   I'm pretty sure (that) . . .
   I have an idea that . . .

3. *Ways of asking for an explanation of an opinion:*
   Why?
   Why do you say/think that?
   What makes you say that?
   What are your reasons (for saying that)?
   Why do you think so?
   Are you sure that . . . ?
   Are you sure of that?
   How come?

4. *Ways of restating someone else's opinion:*
   John thinks/feels/says that . . .
   His/her opinion is that . . .

Activity 1. Learning to Express Opinions

PART A.

When we are talking to other people, quite often we are asked to give an opinion on some topic. The following are some dialogs which illustrate people giving a simple opinion, but without giving an explanation of why they think the way they do. Read through and then practice the dialogs.

1. At school:

        Ann: And what do you think about smoking in class?

    Ricardo: Well, I feel it is unfair to the non-smokers.

2. In a restaurant:

       Jean: How's the steak?

     Peter: Tough.

3. With some friends:

        Ali: What do you think, Grace? Are the Rockets going to win?

    Grace: Personally, I think they'll lose again.

4. In the car:

       Sam: Do you think we can get to our appointment with the doctor on time?

         Di: I'm pretty sure we're not late.

5. At work:

       Kris: I'm not quite sure which is the better plan. What's your opinion?

    Sandy: As I see it, the second plan is a much better one.

PART B.

However, giving a simple opinion is often not enough. People expect us to support our opinion. So, let's look at the same dialogs again, but this time notice that the second speaker supports his/her opinion with an illustration of a fact to back up the opinion.

1. At school:

        Ann: And what do you think about smoking in class?

    Ricardo: Well, I feel it is unfair to the non-smokers because they have to breathe the polluted air from the smokers.

2. In a restaurant:

       Jean: How's the steak?

     Peter: Tough. I can't even cut it.

3. With some friends:

        Ali: What do you think, Grace? Are the Rockets going to win?

    Grace: Personally, I think they'll lose again. Their best player was injured and isn't playing tonight.

4. In the car:

> Sam: Do you think we can get to our appointment with the doctor on time?
>
> Di: I'm pretty sure we're not late. The four o'clock news had just begun when we left.

5. At work:

> Kris: I'm not quite sure which is the better plan. What's your opinion?
>
> Sandy: As I see it, the second plan is a much better one because it costs less and does more for the company.

Activity 2. What's Your Opinion?

Now it is your turn to practice giving opinions. Work in pairs and ask your partner what he/she thinks of a certain topic. Choose several topics from the list below, find out your partner's opinions and write them down so that you will be able to tell the class what your partner thinks and why.

After you have done this, switch roles; that is, you will answer the questions your partner asks you. Make sure you use the expressions you've learned and that both of you give a reason for your opinion each time.

List of topics

fast foods	dogs
television	pizza
dieting	travelling
nuclear energy	neighbors
rock music	winter
city life	various sports: hockey, football,
country life	baseball, skiing
home cooking	history
classical music	hot weather

When your teacher asks you to tell the class what your partner thought, use one of the following forms:

Wai Fong feels/thinks/says that eating certain foods causes cancer because . . .

Her opinion is that certain foods can cause cancer because . . .

Activity 3. Cookie Evaluation Committee

The Krumbel Cookie Company has invited you to come and give your opinion about three new cookies that they have created. You will be one of the three people on the committee, and you will have to decide which cookie is the best.

You should give your opinion on each cookie and using a scale from 3 (very good) to 1 (bad), fill in the chart below. The cookie with the highest score will be the cookie that will be sold to the stores. Remember, when you give your opinion, use one of the expressions you learned earlier in this Unit and support your opinion by giving a reason based on taste, smell, shape, packaging and price.

	Cookie #1	Cookie #2	Cookie #3
Taste			
Smell			
Shape			
Packaging			
Price			
TOTAL (15)			

Activity 4. What Do YOU Think About . . . ?

You should be ready to give your opinion quickly when asked for it, and you should also be ready to give reasons for your opinion. You will be asked your opinion on various things. Be sure to use the expressions you have learned in this Unit.

WHAT DO *YOU* THINK?

Activity 5. A Debate

In this activity, you will have a chance to take part in a debate. What is a debate? It's a formal discussion (argument) between two groups. One group argues for the positive side, and the other argues for the negative side. After this, the rest of the class gets to vote on which group presented their argument better.

First, the teacher will split the class into two groups, and, on different days, each group will hold a debate on the topic of their choice. Half of the group will argue for, and half will argue against the topic. You must decide who will be the first speaker and who will be the second speaker in your group.

Some expressions you may want to use to help you start talking about your topic are:

I feel . . .   I'm certain that . . .
I believe . . .   I'm convinced that . . .
I think . . .   In my opinion, . . .
         Not everyone will agree with me, but . . .

For example, you could say, "I believe that children should not be allowed to watch television until they have done their homework."

*   *   *

Some example topics for debate:
Everyone should spend at least three years living in a different country.
Men with beards are untrustworthy.

Think of some more!

UNIT IX — PERSUADING

Activity 1. A Trip Down Niagara Falls, Anyone?

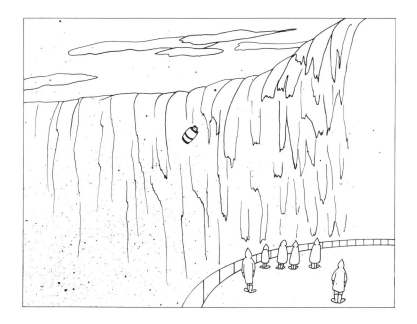

THE CHANCE OF A LIFETIME! A trip down Niagara Falls in a wooden barrel. The barrel is fully furnished with a mattress and a pillow so you can enjoy your trip down the river and the Falls itself. As well, we will include a bottle of clean Niagara River water to drink if you get thirsty on this adventure-packed, once in a lifetime trip. DON'T MISS IT! ONLY $100.00, prepaid of course.

Do you want to go on this trip? Why or why not?

Now look at this ad.

FIRST TIME EVER — FOR ONE MONTH ONLY
SUPER SUBSCRIPTION SERIES
THE WORLD'S GREATEST MUSIC FOR $45.00

You get four concerts for the price of three. Don't miss out on the greatest entertainment opportunity of the year.

DON'T DELAY — CALL TODAY

What are the persuasive features of the ad?

Activity 2.   Okay, I'm Convinced!

Here are some dialogs illustrating different ways of persuading. Read them and try to see how one person persuaded the other to do something.

1. *Situation:* A brother and sister take turns doing the supper dishes. Uri tries to persuade his sister to do the dishes on one of his nights.

    Uri: Leah, would you do the dishes for me tonight?
Leah: No way!
    Uri: I'm supposed to meet the gang early tonight.
Leah: You know it's Tuesday and my favorite TV program's on.
    Uri: Look, I'll do the dishes two extra times. Please!
Leah: I don't know . . .
    Uri: And besides, I'll give you $1.00 when I get this week's allowance.
Leah: Oh, all right. I'll wash the dishes.

How did Uri persuade Leah?

2. *Situation:* Mr. Lim is shopping for a new television set.

Salesperson: This model is more expensive, sir, but it is a better buy in the long run.
    Mr. Lim: Well, there is a hundred and fifty dollar difference, and they both look the same, except for the brand name.
Salesperson: That's true, but with this model you have a longer warranty; if new parts are needed, you do not pay for replacements; and finally, it is produced right here, so there is no waiting for spare parts.
    Mr. Lim: Okay, I'm convinced. I'll take it.

How did the salesperson convince Mr. Lim?

3. *Situation:* Two children are arguing about the location of Rwanda.

Roberto: Sheila, you're wrong. Rwanda's not near Mexico.
  Sheila: Yes, it is. I learned about it at my old school.

Roberto: Well, I read yesterday that it's in Africa.

  Sheila: No, you're wrong. It's definitely near Mexico — my father said so too.

Roberto: I guess I didn't read it right.

How did Sheila persuade Roberto?

*   *   *

Now complete the dialogs. Here are the first lines of each.

Work in pairs and complete the dialog in a different way from the example.

1. Uri: Leah, would you do the dishes for me tonight?

_____

_____

_____

_____

_____

2. Salesperson: This model is more expensive, sir, but it is a better buy in the long run.

_____

_____

_____

_____

_____

3. Roberto: Sheila, you're wrong. Rwanda's not near Mexico.

_____

_____

_____

_____

_____

Activity 3. Learning Persuading Words .

Sometimes people do not respond to an idea as you would like them to. If that happens, then you must try and persuade them. Here are some useful expressions to use after you have heard their objections.

I'll do X if you'll do Y.
Wouldn't it be better if . . .
How about . . .
Well, look at it this way . . .
Yes, but . . .
Sure, but . . .
Okay, but . . .
That's (probably) true, but . . .
That's a good idea, but . . .
I see your point, but . . .
Look, there are many reasons why, but . . .
And besides, . . .
Possibly, but . . .
You might do X.

Examples:

1. Steve: It would be better if we went to the park. It's a much nicer place for a picnic.
    Pam: That's true, but the others are expecting us at the beach.
2. David: You must finish this typing today. I really need it for tomorrow morning.
    May: I'll finish it today if you'll do the laundry.

Now, working in pairs, prepare two or three examples of your own.

Activity 4. Create your Own Dialog

Working in pairs, pick any relationship and any situation and create a discussion, with one person trying to persuade the other to do something he/she did not particularly want to do at the beginning. By the end of the discussion, the second person should agree.

RELATIONSHIPS	*SITUATIONS*
parent/son	buying clothes (or other items)
parent/daughter	choosing a restaurant, place of interest
wife/husband	TV program, radio station
sister/sister	vacation spot, film
sister/brother	how to learn English
friend/friend	how to do homework: in front of the TV or
classmates	in a quiet room
neighbors	which toothpaste to use

RELATIONSHIPS	SITUATIONS
teacher/student	quitting smoking
boss/employee	going on a diet
secretary/boss	joining a fitness class
doctor/patient	joining a tennis club
	going abroad to work
	choosing a wife/husband
	staying out late at night
	sharing housework
	spending too much money
	using the car

Activity 5. Newspaper Ads

Here are three sets of ads. Working in pairs, begin by picking one set of ads, and try to persuade your partner that your product is better. Remember to listen to your partner's reasons and then show him/her why yours is better.

1. *Two Ads for Unfurnished Houses*

> **CENTRAL** — 2 bedroom + den, modernized, 5 new appliances, 2-car parking, $700. mo.

> **VALLEY PARKWAY** — beautifully furnished, 3 bedroom semi-detached townhouse, broadloom, appliances, fenced backyard, private garage, $600. per month.

2. *Two Ads for House Paint*

> **SHINE-IT** — it's smooth; it's creamy, never lumpy; dries quickly rain or shine; now in 50 colors; the paint of the future.

> **COLOR BRITE** — the best in color selection; the only quick-drying paint which *does* dry quickly; easy to apply; non-drip; guaranteed for five years.

3. *Two Ads for Television Sets*

> **TELESITE** — highest technology; excellent picture quality; very down to earth price; fully remote controlled; good sound; five year warranty.

> **VIEWBEST** — ten year warranty; best in sound and vision; various sizes; all fully remote controlled; can be used with many video systems.

74

Activity 6. Hello, Father

Situation: Pedro has received a letter from his father. After he reads the letter, he phones his father. As you can see, they do not see eye to eye on some points. You will work in pairs and play the parts of Pedro and his father. Each one will try to persuade the other that his decision is the best choice.

1157 Esperanza St.,
Oshkosh, Obania.
May 12, 198 –.

Dear Pedro,

Thank you very much for your letter which arrived yesterday. I was pleased to learn that you are happy studying English in Fort York, but I still think that you are making a big mistake. I know that you want to remain in North America and go to university there, but we want you to come home.

If you came home, Mom and I would look after you, cook for you and do your laundry. You would never feel lonely because Mom is home all day, and this would make life very easy for you.

In addition, I cannot understand why you need to go to university, and especially to study philosophy. I never went to university, and I'm not short of money! What kind of job can you get as a philosopher?

In my opinion, you should come home and stop dreaming of nonsense like university study. You can come and work with me in our store. I am sure you will make a lot of money, and one day, when I retire, the store will be yours.

Finally, we want you to get married, and we know so many nice girls here.

Please call us collect as soon as you get this letter.

Love,

Father.

Activity 7. Lost on the Moon

This is a survival game. Each of you picks a role and then your aim is to persuade the group that you should accompany the captain. Remember to use the persuading expressions to help you.

Game:

You are on a rocketship returning to Earth. However, something is wrong with the engines, and you are forced to land on an uninhabited part of the moon. There is some food and drink on board that will last five days if you all stay in one place.

The captain is sure that there is a research station northwest of here, and he is willing to lead a group there. However, he can only take two of you in the space buggy. You must begin by deciding who should go and who should stay. After that, you must decide how to divide up the food. Remember that none of you wants to stay because it is the stormy season on the moon with extreme temperatures and danger from the winds, which makes it frightening.

The people:

1. Captain Hero: 40 years old; loves all kinds of sports.
2. Miss Lola: 23 years old; famous movie star; a university graduate.
3. Miss Prune: 54 years old; history teacher; expert hiker.
4. Dr. Soma: 30 years old; brilliant young physicist; chain smoker.
5. Samantha Love: 60 years old; famous poet; vegetarian.
6. Jonah Tim: 35 years old; well-known chef; hobby is building racing cars.
7. John Dogg: 47 years old; veterinarian; avid stamp collector.
8. Al Engineer: 32 years old; bright engineer; very nervous.

After you have chosen your roles and decided who goes with the captain, you divide the food.

The food:

25 l. water (6½ gals.)	3 tins evaporated milk
5 tins biscuits	2 doz. oranges
3 kg. dried meat sticks (6½ lbs.)	4 doz. chocolate bars
3 kg. dried fruit and nuts (6½ lbs.)	2 very ripe bananas

After you finish, be prepared to tell the rest of the class what your group decided to do.

Activity 8. The Inheritance

You are one of five brothers and sisters. You have just been told that your great uncle has left you an inheritance of $75,000. But, he insisted that you may not divide up the money, and you must all agree to do one and only one thing with it.

Think what you would do with the money, and persuade your brothers and sisters to agree with you.

UNIT X. DEVELOPING AN IDEA

Key Words and Expressions

Look at the following words and expressions which we use to hold our ideas together.

1. *What you say when you want to add information:*
   and
   in addition
   besides
   another thing
   also
   as well

2. *What you say when you want to say the "opposite":*
   but
   however
   although

3. *What you say when you are giving a lot of reasons or facts:*
   first
   second
   third
   then
   next
   finally

4. *What you say to show that this will be an example:*
   for example
   that is
   such as
   for instance

5. *What you say when you want to end off:*
   so
   to summarize
   to sum up

Now look at the two descriptions. Description A has none of these words that hold the description together. Description B uses these words, and this makes it better.

A	B
This is our grammar book. It explains the grammar points. It gives many exercises on how to use words. It teaches us how to use the word "since." There are many exercises for practice. It is a very useful book.	This is our grammar book. *Besides* explaining the grammar points, it gives many exercises on how to use words. *For example*, it teaches us how to use the word "since." *In addition*, there are many exercises for practice. *So* it is a very useful book.

Now you try and make little descriptions like *B*, using words and expressions that we've just learned.

Activity 1. Connecting

In English, we often use connecting words such as:

first, second, third, then, next, finally, when we want to make what we're saying clearer. We use these words especially in three kinds of speaking:

(a) When we are giving a lot of *reasons* for something
(why I love jogging; why I never watch television, etc.)

(b) When we are giving the *rules* for something like a game
(the rules of basketball, chess, etc.)

(c) When we are telling the steps in how to do something or how to use something
(how to make a cake; how to fix an electric plug; how to use a dishwasher, etc.)

Look at this example:

How to Make a Phone Call from a Pay Phone

First (of all), you put a coin into the telephone. *Second,* you listen for the dial tone. When you hear it, *then* you dial the number. *After* the phone rings, someone will probably answer it, and the *next* step is to talk to the person you called. *Finally,* when you have finished, hang up.

Now, working in pairs, you and your partner should each choose one subject from each of the three lists below, and you should tell your partner about the subject. Try to make at least five points on each.

(a) *Giving lots of reasons*
   1. Why everyone should study English
   2. Why smoking is dangerous
   3. Why winter is better than summer
   4. Why summer is better than winter
   5. Why men should/should not carry things for women
   6. Why women should/should not carry things for men
   7. Why salt is bad for you
   8. Why television is important
   9. Why flowers are important
   10. Why computers should be cheaper

(b) *Giving the rules for something*
   1. The rules for asking someone to marry you
   2. The rules of any sport
   3. The main rules for driving a car
   4. The rules for using a swimming pool
   5. The rules for how to write a letter in English
   6. The rules for how to behave when you visit a stranger in this country

78

(c) *The steps on how to do something*
 1. How to make a salad/sandwich/hamburger/cake
 2. How to use a tape recorder
 3. How to make a fire for a barbecue
 4. How to plan a surprise party
 5. How to choose a house to rent/buy
 6. How to choose where to study
 7. How to ride a bicycle
 8. How to become rich
 9. How to become famous
 10. How to train a dog

Activity 2. Scrambled Pictures

In this activity, each person in your group will be given a different picture. Together the pictures make up a story. Do not show your picture to anyone.

You must each describe your picture to the group. Then show your picture to the group and put the pictures in order to make a story. Plan to tell the story that goes with your pictures. Try to make it interesting.

Finally, one person in the group will tell the full story to the class.

Activity 3. Guessing Game

As you can see, there are pictures of many things. You are going to work with another student. Each of you will take turns, and talk about one of the items on the page. Remember how we learned to describe objects in Unit VIII. The other person will then guess which item you are talking about. Do not interrupt while the other person is talking; wait until he/she is finished before you guess, and if you have any doubts, ask questions. Have fun!

Activity 4. Spontaneous Talk

Working in groups of three, each one of you will take turns giving a talk. These talks do not need preparation. You will pick a topic out of a bag, and then you will give your talk on the subject chosen. Try and use the expressions you have learned in this Unit.

If the person speaking stops, help him/her with questions such as:

Tell me a little more about X.
What happened next?
How did you feel?

Your questions should get the person to speak more about the topic.

Activity 5. Making a Picture Story

You will work in groups. The aim is for you to create a picture story with at least five pictures, like the one below:

In your groups you should follow these steps:

1. Decide on the story.
2. Decide on what has to be in each picture in order to "tell" the story.
3. Draw the pictures — at least five! It doesn't matter if none of you can draw well — it just adds to the fun.
4. Give your picture story to the group next to you, and they'll give you theirs.
5. Decide on the story based on the other group's pictures.
6. Meet with the other group and you tell them *their* story and they'll tell you *yours*.
7. See how similar your original story was to the way they told your story.

Activity 6.   Let's Build a Story

You will work in groups.

Once your group gets together, these are the steps that you follow:

1. Choose a topic for a story.
2. Each of you thinks up a sentence on that topic.
3. After you finish your sentences, listen to all the sentences and put them in logical order. If there are similarities, make changes and adapt the sentences. The aim is to build one story out of the sentences. If necessary, add a beginning and closing sentence.
4. Use the expressions that you learned to connect your sentences, so that you will end up with a complete story.
5. As a group, correct the grammar of each sentence.
6. When your story is ready, you will tell it to the rest of the class.

Each group will have a story to tell.

Activity 7.   A Game: Telling a Story

This is a game. Together the class will tell a story. When you are asked to speak, try to make the story as interesting or as funny as possible.

You must speak for at least 30 seconds, and then stop and tell another student to carry on.

NOTE: The story is not serious. It is meant to be fun!

Activity 8.   The News

On-going Activity

Two of you will report on the news every day. One should talk on some international news, and one should talk on some local news.

You should prepare your report at home, but do not write it out — only write down points!